DOING BUSINESS with GOD

BY

KATIE HORNOR

ISBN: 978-1-7346046-7-2, printed in the USA.

CONTENTS

STUDY SCHEDULE

If participating in the LIVE study program, please finish the video, reading and assignments prior to the group call so that our discussion can have full participation.

Here is a suggested study schedule:
Day 1: video
Day 2: *Faith Like Flamingos* (FLF) chapter and study guide
Day 3: *FLF* chapter and study guide
Day 4: *FLF* chapter and study guide
Day 5: *FLF* chapter and study guide
Day 6: *FLF* chapter and study guide
Day 7: attend the live discussion

FACEBOOK GROUP

This is where you can ask your questions and share your wins and takeaways throughout the course, and you're welcome to remain in the community as an alumni after completion of the course as well.

Click this link to join now with the email address you used to purchase the program.

https://www.facebook.com/groups/2224502107784858

IMPORTANT

We require a high level of trust and confidentiality within the Facebook group and the live calls/replays. It is to be a safe place to share struggles and praises, personal and business information. Anyone who does not respect this guideline and betrays the confidence of the group, will be removed from the Facebook group and future group calls without notice or appeal, though you will still have access to course materials. This is necessary to protect the privacy rights of others in the group. By joining the Facebook Group you consent and agree to these confidentiality terms.

TEXT BOOKS
We are using one book along with this study guide for the program. Get your copy of the *Faith Like Flamingos* free ebook download or for-purchase physical books can be found here:

www.TheFlamingoAdvantage.com.com/books

0.

INTRODUCTION

The world, as we know it, is changing. And just as those in my grandparent's generation remember where they were when they heard the news of Pearl Harbor, and those of my parent's generation remember getting their first personal computer in the early 80s, and my generation remembers where we were when we heard the news of the 9/11 attacks on the World Trade Center... so our children's generation will always remember where they were when the world shut down for a global pandemic in 2020.

Much as we wish it were otherwise, after events such as these that touch us so deeply and intimately as a culture and as individuals, things will never be the same.

And yet, in a shaky world, it is possible to have unshakable clarity as to what God wants for you and your business. It is possible to know the formula for consistent peace and to have a system that allows you to make confident decisions based on your faith and God's plan for you. I can't wait to tell you all about it in this study.

I'm Katie Hornor, a woman of faith, a wife, a mom, a business coach and entrepreneur with over 20 years of ministry and business experience. And since 2014, I've been teaching small business owners, teachers, coaches, course creators, and service providers how to overcome their fears and grow their businesses through the power of God's truth.

I believe every challenge you face is a pivot point and an invitation to know God better, to embrace his promises for your future, to step into his plan to use you in the kingdom.

Having taught the material presented in this study to thousands of believers in business, I can say that 99% of the Christian entrepreneurs I've met want confidence, peace of mind and results in their business. And I can say with 100% surety that those things are only achieved by doing business with God, not apart from him.

I truly believe there is no better time than right now, as a believer in the marketplace to learn how applying God's principles to your business will give the clarity, confidence, and vision needed to embrace the unique part you play in his kingdom plan to grow your small business and to grow your impact for Christ in the world.

The days are short, your message matters, and people need what you have to offer. So if you're ready to hear from God about your business, and really grow this thing, join me as I teach you to do business with God.

Stay Teachable. You may have heard some of this before, but because it's coming from God's word, we know that God's word is powerful and living and you, He may have something new to teach you today from something that you've heard before.

Even if you've heard it before, I want you to ask the Lord to open your heart and to teach you something new from what you're hearing. Some people will say "This doesn't apply to me." To which I answer: God's word does apply to you because you are his child, period. His word applying to you has nothing to do with the actual difference in how you serve him. That is the practical application part.

But the principles from God's word apply to you, no matter what business he's called you into. So don't get hung up on that. Ask the Holy Spirit to show you how this applies to you and how you can walk this out in your daily business.

"I BELIEVE EVERY CHALLENGE YOU FACE IS A PIVOT POINT AND AN INVITATION TO KNOW GOD BETTER, TO EMBRACE HIS PROMISES FOR YOUR FUTURE, TO STEP INTO HIS PLAN TO USE YOU IN THE KINGDOM. "

From $5 in a foreign country to six-figures in a pandemic.

So how did I learn about doing business with God? I'm so glad you asked!

My husband Tap and I came to Mexico back in 2007 as missionaries (yes, at the time of this writing, we travel a lot but we're still based here). But at that time we had just spent two years driving around the US and inviting people to support us and send donations so that we could work at a Bible college.

About two years into that, the Lord moved us from there to Campeche, Mexico. Which is way at the bottom of the Gulf of Mexico, right near the Cancun Peninsula.

We came to work at a children's home and we thought that was a forever move. It was a hard move and there were some complicated things that happened when we moved, because we didn't just change ministries, we changed mission boards. And we changed a lot of things and went through a lot of hurt along with that.

The ministry that we left wasn't really happy that we left, to put it lightly, and we ended up losing emotional support and a lot of financial support through that move. However, we knew God was calling us to the children's home. We thought we would be there forever taking over this work for a widowed missionary woman; shepherding that children's home into the future, whatever God wanted that to look like.

But... nine months into it the veteran missionary told us that her national staff wasn't on board with her decision to bring us in as leadership and we needed to leave. Just like that. In a matter of less than 12 months, we'd had two ministry changes. People lost faith in us, and stopped supporting us.

At the same time, there was a money crisis in the States. As the economy crashed it became convenient for churches to say, "Oh, well, you know, you failed. We're not supporting you anymore." Eventually we reached a point where we didn't know from one month to the next what was coming in. We had five dollars left in the bank and literally couldn't get back to the States, even if we'd wanted to. We had four children under the age of five and we were asking the Lord, what do you want us to do?

We had been operating for so long under a fear of man, constantly asking "Who's going to stop supporting us if we do X, Y, or Z, if they don't agree with it?" that we really didn't know what it meant to follow God's leading.

Over the next few months and years, as we started our own business under incredible criticism. Now we were being criticized for being missionaries and working a business. The Lord really had to teach us who he was, and what that meant for us, and what that meant for our children, and what that meant for our business, and what that meant for people we serve.

Everything that I'm teaching you here has come through the fire. We have walked it; we have lived it. We now teach it to our clients.

In 2011, we started a company that was the first, and for a long time, the only literature-based homeschool curriculum company that existed in the Spanish language. Our curriculum provided materials to homeschool children from preschool through sixth grade in Spanish.

"EVERYTHING THAT I'M TEACHING YOU HERE HAS COME THROUGH THE FIRE. WE HAVE WALKED IT; WE HAVE LIVED IT. WE NOW TEACH IT TO OUR CLIENTS."

Then, the Lord allowed us to host the very first in history that we know of, online homeschool summit for Spanish-speaking families. The second year we had over 5,000 families from around the world attend that virtual summit and get encouragement and training.

In 2014 we started coaching Christian entrepreneurs, in 2020 we started hosting virtual Christian Marketing Retreats a few times each year, then added consulting for event strategy. The Lord kept providing the mentors and the resources and the clients and we kept growing.

We thought we'd be a little 30 person ministry in the middle of nowhere in Mexico that nobody had ever heard of, forever. And now we have a ministry that reaches around the world.

The Lord has been faithful through every single step. Then he allowed us to take what we'd learned, like in first Timothy

Two, where you take what has been taught to you and teach it to faithful men–people who will be able to teach it to others as well. That's what this is all about.

In 2017, I was able to synthesize what the Lord had been teaching us in terms of how to do business from a biblical perspective, and how to do business from a people first perspective. That became Doing Business with God. We've taught this program every year since then, seeing it change lives and businesses just as I fully expect it to change yours.

I have a Bible based approach in my coaching and business. I don't just use "Jesus terms" in my marketing, I use it in every class we have. Our believe entrepreneurs must learn more about who God is, because that is the basis of everything that we do in life. And how to evaluate what you do in your business, or if you don't have one yet, how to evaluate where you want to go and how God is leading that.

Knowing God helps you make decisions with confidence, clarity and purpose so that you can be the best at what God has called you to do.

All of us are called, practically, to serve the Lord in different areas. But the thing that we have in common is that we've all been called to bring him glory through the talents that he has given and the business he's entrusted to our care.

1.

WEEK ONE

Day one - **watch** the week one video.
Journal your thoughts here.

Day two - read *Faith Like Flamingos* Intro and Chapter one. **Then complete** the following reading and assignment.

Maybe you've been doing business by yourself for a while. Maybe you've been trying to please other people, or maybe you've been working *for* God, but not *with* him. You need more time to dig in and to study and to figure out exactly what this looks like as you walk it out in your life.

I want to invite you to go deeper.

Do the work, and you will know God more deeply than you ever have in your life this far. You can know God more than you have ever known him in your life. You're going to practice walking in the peace of God because knowing him brings peace. That's what 1 Peter 1:2 tells us; peace and grace are multiplied to you in the knowledge of God. Practice walking that out in your life with your family, and in your business.

You're going to increase energy and passion because it's clear where God is leading you. You're going to be able to choose your work hours. If this is your own business, be able to put those priorities clearly into place, and learn the systems and the processes that you need to guard so that you can do what he's called you to do on both the family front and the business front.

"GOD DOESN'T CALL US TO BUSINESS JUST TO LEAVE OUR FAMILY IN THE DUST. HE CALLS US TO BLEND ALL OF THAT TOGETHER."

God doesn't call us to business just to leave our family in the dust. He calls us to blend all of that together. Some people say *you've got to balance* business and family. God says, "No, *you get to blend* it. This is who you are. And I want you to blend all of that into one beautiful, beautiful act of worship for me."

You're going to learn how to do that. You're also going to know how to keep your thoughts in the right place, no matter what happens. Perhaps you deal with fear or with anxiety. With crazy emotional things because you don't have a system that helps you think on the truth... **Doing Business With God** gives you that system. And it gives you practice implementing that system so that you can think on the truth, no matter what is thrown your way. Then, based on the truth, you'll be able to make decisions and take action, knowing that you're following what God wants you to do next. You're going to know how to implement this with clarity to take action in confidence that you're aligned with what God expects for you and for your business.

I grew up in the mountains of North Carolina and every summer we'd have a revival week. People would come to the nightly revival meetings and get right with God. People would make decisions, "re-dedicate" their lives, but by the next week, and for sure by the next summer, we would need it again.

I don't think God likes us to live that way. We have to put what we've learned and experienced into action. Take what you get in this program and put it into practice. Make it a habit, make it a lifestyle, make it something that is part of your everyday life - every day.

You want to be different. You want to live differently. You want to make a difference. That can happen.

My goal is that the world would be such a world where the small businesses that belong to faith-based business owners end up being the standard of excellence and the beloved first choice in the marketplace because of the way we do business. Because of the way we love people. Because of how they see Jesus in us. God has put me in a position now with the knowledge and the experience that I have to be able to teach you how to do that.

God is bringing this right to you to ask him to help you take that next step. You need to go deeper. You need practice. You need to make this a habit. You need to apply what you've learned and make it a new habit, a new lifestyle in your life so that whenever something happens, your first thought is, "What does God say? What is the truth? And based on the truth, what does He want me to do next? How do I take a step that will glorify him?"

Living in Awe. Why do I need to know who God is? Why does that need to be the basis of my business? Because this is crucial to your success both in business and in personal life.

What is the foundation of our business? What should it be?

"You cannot begin to grasp even the pressed practical aspects of your business until you walk in the fear of the Lord." - Jeff Testerman, *Bible Based Business*

"YOU CANNOT BEGIN TO GRASP EVEN THE PRESSED PRACTICAL ASPECTS OF YOUR BUSINESS UNTIL YOU WALK IN THE FEAR OF THE LORD." - JEFF TESTERMAN

That's really what it's all about. Fearing, having a reverential awe of God.

Until I know who God is, what he's capable of, and how that applies to me personally, I can't apply it to my business. Until I know him and what his principles are for doing life and business, I can't operate by them. And if I'm not applying God's rules in God's ways, there ultimately will not be God's success in what I'm doing. So the fear of him means that our actions and our words are not dictated by what others will think of us, but by what *God* will think of us.

"IF I'M NOT APPLYING GOD'S RULES IN GOD'S WAYS, THERE ULTIMATELY WILL NOT BE GOD'S SUCCESS IN WHAT I'M DOING."

I need to be
- more concerned about God's feelings than man's feelings,
- more concerned about God's approval, than man's approval,
- more concerned about God's praise than man's praise.

When I am doing right, he promises blessing. When I am letting the fear of man rule me, when I am living in the fear of what others will say, and not as concerned about God, ultimately, that fear of man becomes an idol in my life.

An idol is anything that takes that primary worship position in my life. If I'm spending more time thinking about what other people are going to think and say, if I am letting their opinions mold my actions and my responses and my decisions, then that has become an idol.

I love this quote by Danielle Tate: "The positive opinions of others are not a prerequisite for success."

That is so true. The only one whose opinion matters is the Lord's. I took me until I was well into my thirties to finally grasp the truth of that one thing. God's opinion is the only one that matters, the only one whose permission and approval I need.

And it's not just fear as in being afraid of him, but it's more of a reverential awe, the thing that inspires you and blows your mind that God is so awesome and so big and so powerful and yet cares so deeply about every little detail in my life and my business. It's that kind of fear. It's the kind of fear that says, "I may fear what man says and the opinions of other people and what they're going to say about me, but I know God is bigger than that, and I know God has called me to this, and he can handle anything that might happen because of negative responses of other people." That's the fear of God that we're talking about here.

That's the kind of fear that helps us see with clarity what that next step is. That's the kind of fear that says, "Okay, in this instance, I don't see the next step, so I'm just going to keep doing the next right thing, one moment at a time. The next right thing, even though I can't see where I'm stepping. I'm going to have faith in my God to take that next right step, because I know he's called me to this."

In our own life, at the beginning of our ministry in Mexico, we were in a ministry where fear of man was big. You were given jobs to do, with little guidance and then you were either micromanaged, or if you didn't get approval for every little step along the way, there was always something wrong and you were reprimanded for insubordinate or shamed for a wrong decision.

That fear of man became ingrained in us, where we were often afraid of corrections, responses, and criticisms because that's all we ever received. When the Lord brought us to Campeche, Mexico and we could do ministry more on our own, following the Lord, we still kind of had that overarching feeling of having to be careful we didn't upset anyone else by our decisions.

When we changed ministries, we lost a lot of the people who were supporting us, both financially and emotionally in that transition. So, not only had we been ingrained to think we've got to please man to keep doing this, but we also experienced the hurt of people having lost belief in us. We lost our grasp on who God is and because the fear of man was greater than our awe of God. We got to a point where every decision we were making came down to "What are the supporters going to say? How are they going to respond to this?"

When we woke up and realized that this was a very unhealthy place to be living, we had to go back to "Who is my God? Is he bigger than this? Has he called me to this? Can he take care of my needs, no matter what they say or no matter who stops sending financial support?"

And the answer was always yes.

That's your answer too.

God is bigger. And that's when I read again a book called "What do I know about my God?" by Mardi Collier.

In that book is a quote by her husband Ken that says,

"You do what you do and you say what you say because you think what you think, and you think what you think because you believe what you believe about God and his word and yourself."

That is the basis of all of this. If your beliefs are not correct, then your thinking is not correct and your words and your actions and your reactions will not be in line with God and his will for your life. Because this all stems from the heart, from those beliefs that influence our thoughts, that influence our actions and our reactions. All of that comes from our beliefs.

"YOU DO WHAT YOU DO AND YOU SAY WHAT YOU SAY BECAUSE YOU THINK WHAT YOU THINK, AND YOU THINK WHAT YOU THINK BECAUSE YOU BELIEVE WHAT YOU BELIEVE ABOUT GOD AND HIS WORD AND YOURSELF." - KEN COLLIER

So now let's ask: "What do you know about God and why is that important?"

When I know who God is, if I know he has all power, he's strong enough to protect me. Then, can he give me my strength when I need it? Do you see how impactful that could be for my life and my business?

If God has all power and he's always with me, do I need to go through life afraid? No, I don't. Do I need to make business decisions afraid of other people's judgments or reactions or responses? No, I don't.

And if God is good all the time, with no evil in him at all, and he is always good with pure motives, and has all power to control, and he's all good, in all circumstances. I know that whatever he ordains or allows in my life in business is for a good purpose.

Do you see where this is going? Do you see how knowing him makes such a difference as it filters down to our daily decisions based on our belief system?

If I believe God is all knowing—omniscient, and he's all powerful—omnipotent, and he's always present—omnipresent, and he is all good and always good—omni benevolent, then doesn't it make sense that I can trust him?

Good doesn't equal easy.

When I say that God is all good. I don't mean to say that you're going to have an easy life because you believe in him, but I do mean to say that when you know your God as all powerful, all knowing, all present and all good, you have a much greater freedom to walk in his love and share his love and truth with other people in your life and in your business than if you were operating out of fear of man.

Jeremiah 9:23-24 says: "Thus saith the Lord, Let not the wise man glory in his wisdom, neither let the mighty man glory in his might, let not the rich man glory in his riches: But let him that glorieth glory in this, that he understandeth and knoweth me, that I am the Lord which exercise lovingkindness, judgment, and righteousness, in the earth: for in these things I delight, saith the Lord."

So your definition of success is going to look different from my definition of success. It's going to look different from every other person in this Bible study. But the one thing they will have in common is that it will be connected to your God. When you understand and know the Lord, you are successful because when you understand him and you know him and you know who he is and what he expects of you; it gives you the freedom to serve him with all your heart. And that freedom is what will ultimately bring the things that you will consider success in your life.

Success is not a number. It's not a dollar sign. It's not an accomplishment. Every time you reach a goal, have you noticed that you feel good for a minute and then you're onto the next thing? It's because success is not a definite definition and God is saying if you will glory in anything, if there is any honor, if there is any triumph, it's because you know me and you understand my ways and what I want for you.

When we spend time communicating and listening and sharing what we're going through in our daily lives, laughing together, talking together giving, expressing gratitude and praise, enjoying part of another's life. That is what God wants from us.

He wants that relationship where we know him so intimately that he can be part of every aspect of our lives. I've run into people in the business world who have said, "I don't think I can mix my faith with my business."

And I'm saying, "How can you not?" Who you are on the inside is going to show on the outside. And you'll see in the *Faith Like Flamingos* book that we, as believers, are like flamingos. They are pink inside and out. And we are saved to good works inside and out. You can't separate your faith (who you are) from what you do.

Now, you're not going to beat people over the head with the fact that you're a Christian and that you are consulting God's opinion on your decisions for your business. However, it's got to be obvious by the light in your eyes, by the love in your heart, and the value you offer to those you serve, that you are different. That is going to come out. And that daily life part of your faith should not be separated from your business. That should be the thing that draws them in and makes them want to do business with us, because they know we have the character and the integrity and the love for people that makes them *want* to do business with us.

If we don't know God, we will believe the lies that Satan tells us.

What is your definition of success?

In your own words, explain the fear of man.

In your own words, explain the fear of the Lord.

Describe a time when you made a business decision based on the fear of man. What happened? How did it turn out?

What might have been different had you acted on the fear of the Lord instead?

What can you do, or what reminder or boundary can you set for yourself, so that with the next big decision, ou will remember to consider God's desire before making that decision?

Day three - read *Faith Like Flamingos* Chapter two. **Then complete** the following reading and assignment.

How do they train people to recognize counterfeit bills? They train them by showing them the truth. They study the true bills. They memorize every single detail of a true bill so that when they see a fake, they instantly spot the difference.

We need to know God so well. We need to know his truth backwards and forwards so that when we face a lie of the enemy, we can immediately spot the difference: that is not of God and I will cast it out and have nothing to do with it.

Why do I need to go with God? Because I need to be sure that I'm telling others the truth about God. If I don't know it, I can't tell it. If I don't have it in me, if I haven't experienced his grace and truth, I can't share that from a place of vulnerability and from a place of truth with other people.

They don't want to know what you know. They want to know what you've experienced, and if you don't know God, you can't share his truth with them. I need to know God because he has all the answers to life. He's given us everything that we need for life and godliness.

Proverbs 2:1-5 says, "My son, if thou wilt receive my words, and hide my commandments with thee; So that thou incline thine ear unto wisdom, and apply thine heart to understanding; Yea, if thou criest after knowledge, and liftest up thy voice for understanding; If thou seekest her as silver, and searchest for her as for hid treasures; Then shalt thou understand the fear of the Lord, and find the knowledge of God."

Look up the following Scriptures and make notes about what they say regarding why we should know God.
Deuteronomy 4:29
James 4:8a
Collossians 1:10
2 Peter 3:18a

I John 4:10, 19
Ephesians 2:4-5
Jeremiah 31:3
John 3:16
Matthew 22:37
James 4:8
1 John 2:3-5
John 8:44
John 8:31-32
Daniel 11:32b
Job 42:7
Acts 17:28
Proverbs 2:1-5
2 Timothy 3:16
2 Peter 1:2-3
1 Chronicles 29:11-13
Isaiah 43:10b-11
Hebrews 11:6
Psalm 128:1-2
Psalm 119:2
2 Peter 1:2

Day four - read *Faith Like Flamingos* Chapter three. Then **complete** the following reading and assignment.

And what do we find in the knowledge of God?
Second Peter 1:2 says there are two things:
1.
2.

When we have that knowledge of God; when we know who he is, it changes our beliefs, which changes our thoughts, which changes our words, which changes our actions. It changes everything about what we do in our life and in our business. And the result of knowing God is more grace and peace.

Do you know what grace is? There are two different words.

One is defined as "divine enablement." It means supernatural ability to do something that I have to do.

The other definition is "undeserved favor." Now, I know a lot of us pray, "Lord, show me your will. Lord, guide me in your ways." but have you actually asked the Lord for his favor?

My husband started several years ago to ask the Lord for favor in our family prayer time. It was amazing what we began to see. Because not only does it make you realize that God is the giver of all, it also makes you realize that he's willing to give if you ask, and it makes you anticipate finding that favor.

My word of the year that year was rain. Listen for the rain. Look for the blessings. Part of that has to do with favor. My husband continued in our daily family prayer time asking the Lord not only for blessing, not only for guidance and protection, but for his favor, for his unmerited favor, for his grace to do what we need to do. And also for favor in the sight of other people, because that's how God blesses. In Luke 2:52, it talks about Jesus growing up and he "increased in wisdom and stature and in favor with God and man."

"AS I GET TO KNOW GOD, HE HUMBLES ME, AND I SEE HOW FRUITLESS AND USELESS IT IS TO TRY TO LIVE LIFE IN MY OWN STRENGTH AND HOW UTTERLY DEPENDENT I MUST BE ON HIM." - MARDI COLLIER, WHAT DO I KNOW ABOUT MY GOD

So my husband was asking God for favor every day that year, and we saw God do some amazing things. But here's the thing, we don't have to ask him for his favor, because we already have it. What we realized the more we prayed was that we actually needed to ask him to help us *see* the favor he was giving.

Ask God to give you eyes to *see* his favor, to experience the grace and peace that he promises to multiply to you when you know him. He wants to give it to you.

And through the knowledge of God, he has given us all things that pertain to what?

1.
2.

Write out a few of the character qualities of God that stood out to you while reading through this assignment.

Day five - read *Faith Like Flamingos* Chapter four.
Then complete the following reading and assignment.

The enemy has trained us to think in the negative and to be proud and defensive about those things, that God intended to be flaws that would point us to himself and our need of him. When we compare our negative to God's positive, it should uplift us and give us hope. Complete the following opposite statements.

As I see God's greatness, I see my:
As I see God's control, I see my:
As I see God's strength, I see my:
As I see God's holiness, I see my:
As I see God's power, I see my:
As I see God's righteousness, I see my:
As I see God's humility and submission, I see my:
As I see God's giving heart, I see my:
As I see God's wisdom, I see my:

Read aloud and write our 1 Corinthians 10:31

What does this verse mean to you?

Day six - read *Faith Like Flamingos* Chapter five. Then **complete** the following reading and assignment.

Read aloud and write out 1 Thessalonians 5:24.

What does this verse mean for you?

What has stood out to you most in week one's study?

Based on what you've learned about God this week, is there anything in your life or business tat you need to change? Make some note there. Set some deadlines.

In every situation, stop and ask yourself these three questions:

1. What are the facts of the situation?
2. What do I know to be true about my God in this situation?
3. Based on the truths I know, how does my God want me to respond

Let's purpose in our hearts to humbly walk with him, allow him to do through us what he wants done, and be confident, grace-filled and peace-filled as we follow his lead.

Day seven - attend the discussion class or watch the recording.
Record any notes here.

2.

WEEK TWO

Day one - **watch** the week two video.
Journal your thoughts here.

Day two - read *Faith Like Flamingos* Chapter six. **Then complete** the following reading and assignment.

When you are doing business, and business is what God has called you to do, that is a spiritual thing. It is just as spiritual as if you were called into "full-time ministry" because it is a full-time ministry. It's just in a different location than we been taught to prescribe it.

For many of us, that may seem like a new thought, and I want you to think about it, and meditate on the fact that the Lord says in the New Testament that each of us is given different gifts - on purpose.

According to my friend Darren Shearer, in his book *The Marketplace Christian*, those gifts in a business setting may take the form of
administration
apostleship
compassion
connecting
creativity
cross-cultural ministry
business
discernment
encouragement
evangelism
faith
giving
hospitality
intercessory prayer
knowledge
leadership
pastoring
prophecy
service
teaching
wisdom, and more.

All of those gifts work together in the body for the benefit of everyone, for all the believers in the church of Christ. When you are doing the business that God has called you to do, and you are living for him as you do that business, and you are focused on serving him and glorifying him by using your spiritual gifting, and giving your excellence by doing your best, by loving the people that he brings into your path, through your business—that is worship. That is a spiritual job, because that is what he's called you to do.

There's nothing more spiritual than doing what God has created you to do. There's nothing more obedient than doing what God asked you to do. In fact, Jeff Testerman says "For Christians, our business is ministry. It is a part of God's calling in our lives. It's just as 'spiritual' as teach a Sunday school class or preaching a message."

"DOING WHAT GOD HAS CREATED YOU TO DO IS YOUR BEST WORSHIP."

Don't let anyone tell you that you cannot be a Christian in the workplace. Don't let anyone tell you that you cannot mix your faith with your career, because what God has called you to is your **best worship.** It is your service of love to him to do what he's called to do. If you do it with his glory in mind and with his love in your heart, for those people that you are engaging with during the course of that work, that is worship.

For Christians, our business is ministry.

One of my mentors, Jeff Walker, says, "It is your sacred duty to serve the world with your gifts and to overdeliver, because this is the gift you've been given to give the world, whether they buy from you at the end of launch or not."

When we started our businesses after being in full-time ministry for several years, many people had concerns, complaints or questions for us about being in business...

How can you do that?

How can you possibly have time to do both ministry and business?

We found that the Lord multiplied our time because he called us to it and he gave us even more opportunities to minister to others through the business that he gave us.

That's something that I know may be kind of a new thought for you, but I want you to think about it and what it means in your business and to let this truth sink down deep into your heart.

You may have been believing the falsity that you cannot worship God through business, or that a secular career is somehow less than a full-time ministry career. You may have been told that your desires are prideful or that God would not be please for you to do work you desire and enjoy.

My friend, if you are doing what God has created you to do, that is your best worship. It is a spiritual assignment and you can do it with the goal of glorifying God and doing your absolute best to serve him and glorify him through everything that you do in business. Take every opportunity to show Christ to the people in your marketplace.

What do you think about work being worship? What Scriptures can you use to back up your opinion?

Day three - read *Faith Like Flamingos* Chapter seven. **Then complete** the following reading and assignment.

Believers don't separate who we are from our business. We don't separate our faith and our business, or our family and our business. We join them. The idea is blending and not pigeonholing what we do and when.

A flamingo doesn't pretend not to be a flamingo when he's feeding and then go back to being a flamingo when he's flying. That's silly, and yet some Christians think it makes perfect sense to "do church" and "be spiritual" on Sundays and go live like the world the rest of the week, because they think they cannot mix faith and business.

As a child of God who has been entrusted with the care of this business for the profit and purposes of the King, I must bring all of myself everywhere I am and be fully present in that moment, responsive to the Holy Spirit's leading in whatever activity the moment calls for.

Ask yourself this week, "What does it look like for me to blend my secular life with my spiritual life and be who I am authentically, in both places?"

Things die. Death precedes life; a seed buried in the ground has to die before it can bring forth life. Sometimes we have this great idea in our heads and we're all gung-ho and yet the Holy Spirit shuts that door, and we have to say, "Okay Lord, what is it You want? What do You want me to do? Help me hold my ideas loosely until I have the confirmation that they are also your ideas and your will for me." Then you can follow them gung-ho as the Lord brings his plans for you to life. Don't hold on to anything so tightly that God can't do what he wants, because what he wants for you is always better than any of man's imagined ideas that we can come up with on our own.

The world thinks you must separate work and home, secular and spiritual. How is the idea of business as a sacred calling different?

Do you always feel like you're struggling to balance work and family? Separating them to be successful? What if you thought about it as blending instead of balancing? What would blending your Christian beliefs into your business life look like?

What would blending your family life and business life look like?

What is the worst that could happen if you blended these?

Are you afraid of that? If so, why?

Day four - read *Faith Like Flamingos* Chapter eight.
Then complete the following reading and assignment.

One of the big themes in Scripture having to do with life and business is the theme of the farmer. My dad was a farmer. He grew up in upstate New York and they had a dairy farm for many years. So a lot of the stories that I have about farming come from him.

Farming, or sowing/planting and reaping illustrations show God as a creator, God as a God who is in control of all things. God created natural laws that work whether or not you believe in him. They work much better when you do it *with* him. But they will work even if you don't acknowledge him.

The whole idea is that God is your provider. And the more you know him as your provider, the more success you can have in what he's called you to do. What we sow into our businesses God will bless just because of the natural laws. There are natural results that happen when you do certain things, but when you bring God into it and you look at it as God's seed, or God's money or God's time that I'm investing into this, then you can open up a whole new world of greater results and greater impact. That's what we're doing when we run our business *with* God. Knowing who God is, God, as our provider, everything that we do has to come back to who is God.

Our beliefs affect our thoughts, which affect our actions and our words. Essentially, If you are believing wrongly, you will think wrongly. And when you're thinking wrongly, your words and actions are wrong. And then things get all mismatched and mixed up and don't come out the way you intended.

There's an expectation when you plant a seed in the ground that you're going to get something back.

There's an expectation when you put stuff into business that you're going to get something back.

But when we have our wires crossed, in how we're thinking about it or in the way that we're believing about it, then our results get crossed and mixed up, too.

So it's important that we know who God is and how he intends to provide for us. Getting your thinking straight, getting your beliefs solid. That's what we must do i we want success in business. God is sovereign.

Ephesians 1:17-23 talks about God being in control of it all. "That the God of our Lord Jesus Christ, the Father of glory, may give unto you the spirit of wisdom and revelation in the knowledge of him: The eyes of your understanding being enlightened; that ye may know what is the hope of his calling, and what the riches of the glory of his inheritance in the saints, And what is the exceeding greatness of his power to us-ward who believe, according to the working of his mighty power, Which he wrought in Christ, when he raised him from the dead, and set him at his own right hand in the heavenly places, Far above all principality, and power, and might, and dominion, and every name that is named, not only in this world, but also in that which is to come: And hath put all things under his feet, and gave him to be the head over all things to the church, Which is his body, the fullness of him that filleth all in all."

He's our faithful promise keeper, Hebrews 10:23 says "Let us hold fast the profession of our faith without wavering; (for he is faithful that promised;)" -Hebrews 10:23

We talk about God being faithful to fulfill his promises to us. Do you know those promises? Do you know what promises God has made to you? Have you taken time recently to dig into them and see what God has to say about your business? You need to do that. If you haven't yet, go ask, what is God saying about my business?

"Whether therefore ye eat, or drink, or whatsoever ye do, do all to the glory of God." 1 Corinthians 10:31

If everything I do needs to bring God glory, then I need to know what God says about what I'm doing. That's just logic, and it's a biblical principle. But it's much, much more logical even than that. I must know what He requires.

"He hath shewed thee, O man, what is good; and what doth the Lord require of thee, but to do justly, and to love mercy, and to walk humbly with thy God?" Micah 6:8

How can you walk with him? If you don't know him? You've got to know your God.

It is possible to do things well with no knowledge of God and still get good results, because God honors the natural laws of the world. You can study everything. You can study about being a farmer. That was the example we've used. You can have a good crop, and you can make a good profit from that. But when you study everything humanly possible and you rely on the God of the harvest to bless that crop, your results can be even more.

The farmer counts the cost of the sowing, weighs the risk and potential intentionally, sows the seed *expecting* a multiplication in the harvest and then cares for the seed as it grows and multiplies, protecting his investment until it matures.

In our line of work, whatever that may be, we want to do everything that is humanly possible to be excellent in all that we do. We also rely on our God, who knows all and is all powerful, to bless our work. We want to ask him for his creative ideas to do our work well, and for multiplication and blessing. Ask him to let you see the seed multiplied and to see the favor he gives, and be ready to praise him and honor him as he works in your life and business.

Here's another farming thought. A seed has to be left in the ground and die before it can bring forth fruit. The size of something at it's beginning is never a good indicator of it's end. A farmer has to let go of the seed, plant it alone, in a dark place, let it die so that it can be raised to life anew through God's power of sunshine, rain and nutrients. A powerful picture.

What is God asking you to let go of? To let die so that he can birth in you or in your business the new thing he wants to grow through you?

What are some of the natural talents, knowledge or skills God has given you?

What have you done lately (in the last 3 months) to perfect or make more excellent those natural abilities?

What talents do you need to improve for greater impact or income opportunities?

What knowledge or professional development do you need to seek to improve your abilities and opportunities?

How can you partner with God for better results these areas?

Time:

Treasure (finances):

Team:

Trade (products):

Traffic (marketing):

Day five - read *Faith Like Flamingos* Chapter nine.
Then complete the following reading and assignment.

Describe God according to Proverbs 6:16-19.

One of the things we know from this passage is that God hates pride. What is it you're prideful about?

The Bible says pride goes before a fall. What is it you can release that pride for, in order to exchange it for dependence on the Lord?

God hates pride. It's one of the seven things that He hates. He hates pouting, a proud look, a lying tongue, hands that shed innocent blood, a heart that devises wicked imaginations, feet that are swift in running to mischief, a false witness that speaks lies, and he that sows discord among brethren. These are things we can lay aside.

"Sowing discord" is comparing yourself with somebody else, always complaining or gossiping about other people and their successes or their struggles, or intentionally stirring up strife, getting people worked up about non-important matters. Those are things that the Lord hates.

Which of them might you need to ask God's forgiveness for and make different choices going forward so that you avoid offending him by continuing to do these things?

We also see that my God is my father. I love the truth that he has taken me into his family. My God delights in me. He chastens me. He takes care of me. He protects me. He keeps me safe in his hand. This one comes from John 10:29, "My Father, which gave them me, is greater than all; and no man is able to pluck them out of my Father's hand."

When I was little, my dad would come home from working construction all dirty and he often didn't have enough time to shower before dinner was ready. So, instead of sitting on the furniture, because he was so dirty, he would lie down on the floor. When he did, all the change in his pocket would fall out on the floor. I remember as a four or five-year-old running to grab that change. But dad was always faster, and he always grabbed it first. He would hold it in his hand and say, "Katie, if you can open my hand, you can have this money." Well, as a child, I can't physically open a strong man's hand unless he wants me to open it. No way!

That's what I think of every time I hear this verse where God says, no man is able to take you out of my father's hand. But then he goes on to say, "No man is able to take you from the father's hand." So, not only are we safe within the hand of Jesus, but he also says nothing's going to take you out of it. You are not going to lose your salvation, your inheritance, once you have been saved. He says you have become mine, and you have been placed in my hand. Secure. period. end of discussion.

But it's like he knows that we would need more assurance and he goes on to say that beyond that, we have the ultimate protection of his Father God, the One who has us in his hand. There is double protection and that is important for us. No matter what I do in life, no matter what my character is, no matter whether my business succeeds or fails in the world's eyes, no matter whether I'm a good parent or an awful one, no matter whether I have a good day or a bad day, There is absolutely nothing I can do or anyone else can do to me that could take me out of the hand of God and separate me from the love of Jesus, once I have accepted his gift of salvation and I am in his hands.

That is who you are.

You are his.

You cannot do anything else to make him love you any more than he loves you right now, and yet he desires SO much more for you!

When you serve him with excellence; when you serve him with all of your heart, my friend; when you depend on him to bless those efforts that you have done for his glory; that is when God begins to see his favor and blessings on you. That is when he can really grow your business.

When you allow your desires to die so that he can give life to what he wants to give life to through you, that is when God can bless. That is when he can create the miracle of things that you could not have even expected or anticipated in your life. I am living proof of that and he wants you to be as well.

Read the following verses and describe God according to what the verses say about him. What is he like? What does he do?

Psalm 68:5
Psalm 10:14
Ephesians 2:18-19
Galatians 4:4-7
1 John 3:1
2 Samuel 22:20

Day six - read *Faith Like Flamingos* Chapter ten.
Then complete the following reading and assignment.

One thing that I hear a lot from clients is "I'm not enough. I'm not enough to do this." I will just tell you straight out, "You're right. You're not enough."

But that's not harsh, because the truth is God is enough. **God is enough.** And if he has called you to this, this is not about you. It's about him. And if he has called you to this, he has already promised to do through you what he's called you to do.

1 Thessalonians 5:24. "Faithful is he that calls you who also will do it."

That doesn't mean I have to do it in my own strength. That means God's promising to do it through me, if he's called me to this. Jesus didn't call and train preachers and priests to change the world with his message; he called everyday tradespeople. Here's who the leaders of the early church would be if they lived in contemporary times with us:

Peter, John and James—food industry (fishing)
Matthew—IRS/savings and loan manager (tax collector)
Paul—RV manufacturing (tent-making)
Luke—medical doctor
The Seven (Acts 6) —businessmen
The Ethiopian first convert—banker
Dorcas—manufacturer of inner garments
Lydia—upscale clothing material distributor
Cornelius—senior military officer
Simon the tanner—leather goods

I believe God wants you to be the one out there in his marketplace. He wants *you* to be the one. You're the one interacting with people every day in everyday situations, and everyday stresses, and everyday questions, and everyday worries. He wants you to do this.

It's his ministry, and he's called you to this so that he can work through you what he wants to do.

You are not enough, but God is. And he's already promised to do the work he's called you to. He is faithful. You guys, there's never been a moment in our life when he did not provide. I couldn't see it sometimes, but that didn't mean he wasn't providing. I didn't know where the next step was sometimes, but that didn't mean he wasn't already there. I didn't know how it was going to happen, but that didn't mean it wasn't going to happen.

This was God's plan. He said, I will do through you what I've called you to do. I will let God use me. That's what he's asking us. He does the calling. He does the work. He wants us to be willing to let him do it through us.

Read the following verses and describe God according to what the verses say about him. What is he like? What does he do?

Proverbs 3:11-12
Mathew 6:26, 32
John 10:29
Psalm 84:11
1 Thessalonians 5:24

In every situation, stop and ask yourself these three questions:

1. What are the facts of the situation?
2. What do I know to be true about my God in this situation?
3. Based on the truths I know, how does my God want me to respond

Based on what you've learned this week, in your own words, write out a song or prayer of praise to God for WHO he is.

Based on what you've learned about God this week, is there anything in your life or business that you need to change? Make some note there. Set some deadlines. Let's purpose in our heart to

1. Embrace the calling/business to which he has called us.
2. Strive for excellence in as much as we can do in this role.
3. Expect him to (look for him to) supernaturally do his part to complete the work through us.

Day seven - attend the discussion class or watch the recording.
Record any notes here.

3.

WEEK THREE

Day one - **watch** the week three video.
Journal your thoughts here.

Day two - read *Faith Like Flamingos* Chapter eleven. Then **complete** the following reading and assignment.

I think often we misrepresent that verse Psalm 37:4 says, "Delight thyself also in the Lord: and he shall give thee the desires of thine heart."

If you want a better handle on this, read verses 1-9 - the entire passage. This is not saying put God first and then you can do whatever you want. It's saying that if you are seeking God first, if you are walking *with* him, delighting yourself in him, then he is able to place in you the desires that He wants you to have, which are going to be desires he can happily fulfill.

When you are trusting in God, already "doing good things" in his name, committing your way to him, looking for him to prosper your work, resting in him, he will not let you miss those desires he's placed in you. He's not going to let you make a bad decision if your true heart's desire is to serve him and he's going to put those desires in your heart that are things he wants to fulfill. It's almost as if he's saying, "I'm going to make you want this because I want to give that to you." Does that make sense?

God puts those desires in you that he wants you to have so he can give you the desires of your heart. He actually puts those desires in your heart and then he can fulfill them for you. What an amazing truth.

When faced with a decision, if your options are good and good, which do you choose? You choose the one you want because they're both good decisions and God allows us that free will to choose and make decisions. If God is pleased if I do this, and God is pleased if I do this other thing, then what do I *want* to do? You can follow that. If God doesn't want you there, he's going to shut that door. He's going to make it obvious that's not where you're supposed to go. But if not, then you're at complete liberty to choose whichever one of those good options he has placed before you.

Yes, you can seek wise counsel, but also balance that with knowing that *no one else* knows what God is speaking to *your* heart. You don't need another human's permission or approval to obey what God asks you to do.

YOU DON'T NEED ANOTHER HUMAN'S PERMISSION OR APPROVAL TO OBEY WHAT GOD ASKS YOU TO DO.

In my conservative Christian upbringing, I was taught that if I wanted to do something it was probably sinful, and I should repent of my desires and be willing to do what God was going to ask me to do instead - which was probably something I wouldn't enjoy but needed to suffer through to be a "good child of God."

What kind of a picture of a loving God is this? That he would force upon his child something they did not enjoy? I believe now that God's will allows for choices that bring joy - it may not be easy but it will be joy filled.

So, when I was in ninth grade I had a burning desire to serve God overseas somewhere. All of my friends were "surrendering" to serve God on the mission field like it was a fate worse than death they needed to be willing to do. And I was excited about going! It was staying in the U.S. that sounded like doom and gloom to me. So I "surrendered" to stay if that's what God wanted, but I told him that unless he made it super obvious that he wanted me here, my goal was the mission field and I was making every decision from then on with that in mind.

The end of the story is that I married a man heading to the mission field as well. And we have served nearly 17 years on the mission field together. Has it been easy? Not all the time. Has there been joy - most definitely. I believe God put that desire in me, and separately in my husband, so that he could fulfill it and use us on the field in all the ways he has to date.

What is your reaction to this quote by Jeff Testerman (Bible Based Business)? "God has given us the desires of our hearts. What you desire to do and accomplish is there because God has placed it in you."

Describe in detail your dream day?

Now brainstorm how you can make that happen. How could this dream day be every day of your life? And if you're going to get bored with that, then let's throw in things that keep you on your toes and not bored, but describing that dream day... if your day was perfect, what would it look like? And then, how can you make that happen?

Once you define it, you can work for it, make tweaks to get yourself closer and closer to the goal. Let's set those end goals. This is what I want my day to look like every day. And then, how do I make that happen in my business and in my life?

Day three - read *Faith Like Flamingos* Chapter twelve.
Then complete the following reading and assignment.

What do you want your marriage to look like in the future? Take steps now to make that happen. Do you need to have more quality time together? What can you do in your schedule to make that happen? Can you give up an extra dessert a week so you have money for a babysitter one night a week, or can you go for a walk in the park together? You don't have to spend extra money to do that.

What do you want your finances to look like? If you need an extra $2000 a month, where is that going to come from? What can you do?

How many products do you need to sell at $97 each to make an extra $2000 a month? Where's that product going to come from? How can you put it together? How soon can you put it together and get it out there? Who could help you market it? Look at the resources that you have, and the people you know, and brainstorm all of that and put it together.

Your clarity, your vision, and your purpose give you faith: "This is what God has for me." That clarity also helps you make decisions. If something comes as an opportunity for you, you can say, "That doesn't fit with the goal that I have right now, and so I will put it on the back burner, or I will say 'no' for a time because it doesn't fit the direction I'm going in this moment (or for this month, or for this quarter, or whatever it is), to meet this next big goal I believe God wants me to set for myself or for my business."

It may not be a bad idea. It may be a fantastic opportunity, but if it doesn't fit with the goals that God has aligned me with right now, then I can say no with freedom and not feel bad or guilty about saying no to that because it doesn't fit with what God has in front of me right now.

That's where that purpose and vision give you clarity and give you freedom in your business to make those decisions with confidence that this is what God has me doing right now.

I will let nothing detract me or distract me or pull me aside from going in that direction. I have purposed in my heart, like Daniel said, that "I will not defile myself with the King's meat." (Daniel 1:8) Daniel had a vision. He had clarity about what was expected of him and what his goals were, and he wasn't going to let anything pull him away. He had that purpose in his heart and that's what God wants for us in our lives and in our businesses.

Where do you want to be in 6 months or a year from now with your business?

In your relationship to your spouse, what is one thing you want to improve (that you can control - not talking about them or their part) in the next 6 months?

How do you want your finances to be different in 6 months?

Clarity vision and purpose gives faith. Faith is the ability to see the unseen make it a reality. This is why folks create vision boards, so they can "see" the goals they've set for themselves. The visual reminder often brings us back to focus when we wander.

Day four - read *Faith Like Flamingos* Chapter thirteen. Then **complete** the following reading and assignment.

"We were created by God to be goal oriented, to be motivated by having a purpose, to press towards a vision. Are you willing to let God show you his vision for your business?" - Jeff Testerman, *Bible Based Business*

According to this quote, God created us to be goal oriented. God puts that desire in you to meet goals and to meet challenges and overcome them.

We are motivated by having purpose, by pressing towards a vision, but we've got to be willing to let God show us his vision for our business.

Take some time to pray through and write out your answers to the following questions. Be prepared to share them with others who can cheer you on and be a place of accountability.

What goals do you want to reach in six months?

What resources do you have to meet those goals?

Who are the people you know who could possibly help?

What resources do you need?

How can other people help you find those resources?

What is the biggest potential hindrance to you meeting this goal?

And what can you do to avoid that hindrance or make it a non-issue?

What's the result if you don't meet it? Think about that. If I don't get this done at this appointed time, what's going to happen? What's the result of that?

If I do get it done, then how can I reward myself?

Day five - read *Faith Like Flamingos* fourteen.
Then complete the following reading and assignment.

I've always wanted a ring that's made out of a spoon handle, ever since I was a teenager. The ring only costs something like 15 bucks, but I've always wanted one. I'd never had the opportunity to get one.

So, when I published the book, *In Spite of Myself: How Intentional Praise Can Transform Your Heart and Home*, the goal in my heart was to get that book to the bestseller list on Amazon. So I said, "If we make it to the bestseller list with this book, I'm going to reward myself with that spoon ring."

When we launched the book, we did a 12-week launch process with a team of 150 ladies that God just miraculously brought together. And God did it. I don't know how he did it. It defeated all the numbers and statistics and possibilities that normal people have to reach, but the Lord took that book to the bestseller list in the first week on Amazon, and just completely blew the stats and the probabilities out of the water.

The Lord rewarded me with that ring. So, I wear that ring often as a reminder that God can do the impossible, that God can do things that we just have no idea of what he's going to bring for us.

He can do that for you as well, but don't be afraid to set those goals and to set the expectation and plan the celebration. What will I do when I reach this to celebrate and to give God glory and to be a reminder to me in the future of what God can do?

What is the first step for you in meeting the goal you outlined yesterday?

Day six - read *Faith Like Flamingos* Chapter fifteen.
Then complete the following reading and assignment.

God is a good father. Whether or not you had a good earthly father, think specifically about a time when God has shown you, very specifically, that he is good and that he is caring for you and your needs. Write that down here:

I want you to remember this so that when you have hard days, you can go back and say, "This is hard, but look what God did in this last hard time. Look how God came through in this instance. Look how God cares for me. Look at what he did." Your own words and experience will remind your heart of the truth.

Because sometimes it's hard to get our heads out of our immediate situation and we need to be able to remember the things that God has done in the past and say, "If he can do that then I know he's the same God, I know it in my heart. I believe he is the same God. He has the same power. He has the same love for me. He has the same ultimate control of this circumstance. Then I know he is going to care for me in a very detailed way, even in this situation."

God is in control, and we need to be okay with that.

GOD IS IN CONTROL, AND WE NEED TO BE OKAY WITH THAT.

Sometimes we know it in our heart, and we know it in our head, but then we try to take control with our hands. You can't do that. You've got to be okay with whatever God decides is the best for you in this situation. That's not to say go make bad decisions, or make no decisions.

You can't just go around with no backbone and be like, well, whatever happens, happens. No, you have intelligence. You have experience. You have God's knowledge and wisdom. You make the best decisions possible, but realize and believe in your heart of hearts that ultimately God is in control and has either *allowed* or *ordained* every circumstance for your good and for his glory. He will ultimately be your sun and your shield in every situation.

"For the Lord God is a sun and shield: the Lord will give grace and glory: no good thing will he withhold from them that walk uprightly" (Psalm 84:11).

That's you. That's you who are seeking to do your life and your business according to God's ways, and that's his promise for you.

Look up and write out below three verses that remind your heart of the truth that God is in control.

Look up and write out below three verses that remind your heart of the truth that God is trustworthy and wants you to trust him.

Based on what you've learned about God this week, in your own words create a drawing, song or a prayer of praise to him for who he is.

Based on what you learned about God this week, is there anything in your life or business that you need to change? Make some notes here. Set some deadlines.

In every situation, stop and ask yourself these three questions:

1. What are the facts of the situation?
2. What do I know to be true about my God in this situation?
3. Based on the truths I know, how does my God want me to respond

Let's purpose in our hearts to
1. Recognize his divine and perfectly loving control.
2. Rejoice in his detailed care and provision.
3. Remember how he's worked in the past and trust him with the future.

Day seven - **attend** the discussion class or watch the recording.
Record any notes here.

4.

WEEK FOUR

Day one - **watch** the week four video. **Journal** your thoughts here.

Day two - read *Faith Like Flamingos* Chapter sixteen. **Then complete** the following reading and assignment.

This week we're talking about three things: the power of contentment, the power of thinking, and fear of success. We started this whole experience by saying that our beliefs influence our thoughts. It's important for us to believe rightly in order to think right, in order to act and say the things that we're supposed to do and say to bring success in our life and in our business.

The power of contentment.

At the beginning of this study we asked for your definition of success. If you've followed me for any period of time, or heard any of the guest interviews on my *For Your Success* podcast, you know that's a question that I ask people a lot. Everyone has a different definition, and that's okay, because God made us all different. We want to make sure that our definition lines up with God's definition of success, even while it's not required to line up with that of another human.

There are a couple of things that success is not.

Number one, **success is not any amount of money.** It is not achieving a certain career goal. It is not getting certain people to look up to you. Success, as Jeff Testerman defines it, is when you reach a level of personal contentment that puts you in a place of peace and joy. This is something between you and God. And it is something that cannot be bought or sold, and you cannot take it with you when you die.

If you remember that knowing God gives grace and peace: In 2 Peter 1:2 scripture says, "Grace and peace be multiplied unto you through the knowledge of God."

So we're saying success is a level of contentment that has joy and peace with it. How do we get that? We get that through knowing God. Even success in our business can come through that personal relationship with God and knowing who he is. It does not depend on things. It does not depend on other people's opinions. It depends on my relationship with God and my contentment in him. It's accepting who I am in God and knowing that he has accepted me.

Even last week, when you wrote out your outline of what the perfect day looks like, did you realize it's possible to have a perfect day right now because that perfect day means I know who I am with God. I know that he's accepted me. I know I have his favor. I know he created me, with my quirky uniqueness for *his* purpose. I know I'm doing what he wants me to do—and that can give me joy right here in this moment. I am successful, if that is the case.

There are also dangers of being content. What are they? One is laziness. We don't want contentedness to sound like, "Well, I'm good. God loves me as I am. I don't have to do anything." In one sense that is a true statement. We don't serve him to *get* anything. We have as much favor and as much love as he could possibly give us right now. However, we serve him now to show our love and gratefulness to him and to share his glory with others. He created us as people of work. He created us to do and to create and to make and keep commitments that stretch us.

Then, on the other end, as the pendulum swings, there is the danger of overworking. The danger is making our work our God, instead of being content with who God is and the work he's given us to do. It's possible to make work the idol in our lives if we're not careful. Even in this area of contentment, it's not like, "Okay, I'm good. I don't have to do anything." But neither is it doing so much that I forget to take time for God and the other important things that he's put into my life. We want to experience contentment with where we are, but stay dissatisfied enough to keep pushing forward. Not dissatisfied enough to complain or to have a "woe is me" or sorry for yourself attitude, but that dissatisfaction that keeps you pushing for the more that God has for you.

In Scripture, it says to be content with such things as you have (Hebrews 13:5). It says not to care for the things of tomorrow, for the things of tomorrow will take care of themselves (Mathew 6:34). God knows what you need before you ask. Scripture also reminds us not to be lazy, not to be so content that we become slothful and lazy.

Look up the following Scriptures that give us seven steps for experiencing that contentment. Write those down and go through them.

1. Recognize you were bought with a price. 1 Corinthians 6:20.

2. Be thankful for what you have right now. Psalm 100:1-5.

3. Don't compare yourself with others. 2 Corinthians 10:12.

4. Focus on the abundance not the lack. 2 Corinthians 9:6

5. Remember that things don't bring happiness. Jeremiah 9:23-24. Luke 12:15-21.

6. Avoid covetousness traps. Don't put yourself into situations where you know you'll face temptation to desire or lust. Luke 12:15. Hebrews 13:5.

7. Be content with what you have and who you are. 1 Timothy 6:7-9.

We want to think on these things. Which of those things stands out to you the most? Which of those things do you need to work on in order to have that kind of contentment in your life?

Day three - **read** *Faith Like Flamingos* Chapter seventeen. **Then complete** the following reading and assignment.

I grew up believing that working too much was bad, sinful even. That work-a-holism was just as bad as alcoholism and the effects, I was told, on those you love could be just as damaging if one worked "too much".

I'm not sure anyone ever defined what "too much" was, but I interpreted it as wanting to do more because I enjoyed it and so, too much of the thing God commanded us to do - work - was bad.

Then as I grew older I fell into the thinking trap that all work was bad. That I should live for the work free weekends, that I should dread Mondays - and I did.

But then God showed me this verse:

"There is nothing better for a person than that he should eat and drink and find enjoyment in his toil (work). This also, I saw, is from the hand of God." Ecclesiastes 2:24 (ESV).

And I was stunned. I literally studied it for weeks. I couldn't believe in all the Sunday morning, Sunday night, Wednesday night, Revivals, special services, etc that I'd sat through, not a single Bible teacher had ever mentioned *that* verse!

We are to find *enjoyment*? in *work*!?

Wow!

Then I looked back at God's example of Creation in Genesis. I looked as his commands to work and rest, his commands to give honest weights in the marketplace (Deuteronomy 25:15), to lay up an inheritance for your children and children's children (Proverbs 13:22). I couldn't ever find a negative reference to working, creating, tending what God's put in my hands to steward, other than the negative of *not* doing it.

And in discovering that our Creator God gave us all the building block elements with which to work and create things (as opposed to just creating it all for us) I came to believe that he must have known there was enjoyment in the process of discovery, of trial and error, of creation...

73

Which led to asking, then why did he institute the sabbath? "And he said unto them, The sabbath was made for man, and not man for the sabbath:" Luke 2:27.

I believe God designed us to enjoy labor, to enjoy working and discovering, imagining and creating. And I believe that he knew we'd find so much enjoyment in our work - if it is the right work - that we'd never want to stop, therefore necessitating the command of a sabbath. For physical and spiritual rest. For celebration and thanksgiving.

This resulted in me looking hard and long at the kinds of things I was doing for "work". Rescheduling my hours so I could do my work when I was at my peak performance times of the day and week for those tasks. Choosing to do more of what gave me energy and enjoyment and delegating the things that sucked energy or that I dreaded. It even led to me almost eliminating the word "work" from my vocabulary because of the negativity I felt toward the word and replacing it with "business activities." I became very careful of how I spoke about "getting to do business." instead of "having to work."

What has been your view of work? Have you held any wrong beliefs that need to be corrected?

What is the truth that sets you free from those wrong beliefs?

Do you enjoy your work? And if not, why not?

If there is really nothing better that you should "eat and drink and find enjoyment in your work," (Ecc. 2:24) what could you change beginning today to enjoy your work more?

"YOU DO WHAT YOU DO AND YOU SAY WHAT YOU SAY BECAUSE YOU THINK WHAT YOU THIN. AND YOU THINK WHAT YOU THINK BECAUSE YOU BELIEVE WHAT YOU BELIEVE ABOUT GOD, HIS WORD, AND YOURSELF." - KEN COLLIER

D ay four - read *Faith Like Flamingos* Chapter eighteen. Then complete the following reading and assignment.

The power of true thinking.

Are you thinking on truth? Are your beliefs founded in truth? Where's your heart? Are you thinking the right things about God? Is that influencing your thoughts as you go forward in daily life and business?

I found it really amazing that one of the old bible teachers I was reading said that we need to pursue the blessing and favor of God in our lives so that we can become a conduit or a channel of God's blessing to the world around us.

If I'm delighting in God and walking with him, even pursuing his favor becomes not about me. Even God's blessing in our business is not about us, friend. It's about God. It's about us being a channel through which he can reach people, bless people and do his work in their lives.

When we see our abundance as something that is just administered for him, or stewarded on his behalf and for his benefit...

When we see our business as a way to bless others...

When we see money as a *tool* with which to do God's work in the world...

When we see the income and the profit we make as a way for us to do more of that work...

Then he can bless us with more.

Then we have become a conduit, a channel of God's blessing, to the world around us. That's why we pursue his blessing and his favor in our business.

God *wants* to prosper us, but he also wants us to ask. Some have said that a prosperous or "successful" soul means a soul that is mature in Christ which reminds me of Joshua 1:8. Again, it doesn't have to do with money or a bank account number. A "prosperous soul" is a soul that is mature in Christ. Sound in the wisdom of God, full of the love of God, full of love for God's people, full of love for the world. A prosperous soul is also wrapped up fully and completely in God and in his spirit.

"This book of the law shall not depart out of thy mouth; but thou shalt meditate therein day and night, that thou mayest observe to do according to all that is written therein: for then thou shalt make thy way prosperous, and then thou shalt have good success." (Joshua 1:8)

You can look up that verse on biblegateway.com and see 51 different translations just in English. Success is mentioned only in that verse, Joshua 1:8, and in 90% of those 51 translations, it comes up as either *success* or *prosper.* Prosper, meaning to make you do well in all of these things. That is one of the only Scriptures that uses that word success, and he's using it in conjunction with the word prosper. To quote Jeff Testerman again (*Bible Based Business*), "When you have that prosperity of the soul, then you can handle any other kind of prosperity that God brings to you. Focus first on the prosperity of your soul". The other things will prosper as God wants them to.

You focus first on prospering in maturity and in love for God, and in the relationship with him that brings peace and joy, and he will take care of the other things. When you have that maturity, then you can also be blessed with financial blessings and material blessings.

The modern day church needs to correct the way we think about prosperity and the way we think about success in order to handle the success that God wants to give us.

One of my business mentors, Jeff Walker, says that in the business world you want to "knock their socks off with value." You can only ever expect 2% - 5% of your audience to buy from you at a given time. But as Jeff says, it's your "sacred duty" to serve the world with your gifting. You show up and serve them, and you give to the world as much value as you can give, because that is your calling, your duty, regardless of whether they turn out to be part of the 2% who become clients or the 98% who don't choose to right now.

I believe the process towards prosperity of the soul has five parts:

1. Recognize your unique God given strengths and weaknesses.
2. Know who you are in Christ.
3. Learn to live with the future (eternity) in view. Big picture, long game.
4. Rejoice when tested.
5. Exercise self control.

Look up and write out 2 verses to support each of the above steps:

Which of these do you most need to focus on maturing over the next month, by God's help?

How has God uniquely positioned your business to be a conduit of his blessing to others?

Day five - read *Faith Like Flamingos* Chapter nineteen. Then complete the following reading and assignment.

Fear of success.

Something I see in a lot of Christians in business and Christian entrepreneurs is that many of us are afraid of success. Maybe we're afraid of the judgment and scrutiny that comes when we're successful. Maybe we're afraid of what others are going to say about us when we're successful. Maybe we're afraid of losing family or friends who don't understand our success or feel entitled to a part of it by sheer proximity.

There are a lot of things that you can be afraid of when it comes to success. But one thing that we can know as truth from Scripture is that **my God does not want me to be afraid.**

We need to purpose in our hearts to be content, but also to purpose in our hearts to anchor ourselves in hims so we have courage toi anticipate the growth that God wants to send. We need to believe that he is who he says he is in his word, and that he will do what he says he's going to do. We need to take those thoughts and those imaginations captive when they rise up and threaten to choke out the true beliefs that we have in our hearts about God. We need to compare all of those thoughts and those doubts and those things that are thrown at us to his word before we accept them as truth.

Don't just accept any thought that comes to your head as truth. Don't just take anything someone says to you randomly as truth. Go back and compare it to Scripture before you decide what you're going to believe in your heart to be true, and base your thoughts and actions on truth.

Embrace your talents and skills. Embrace your quirks. Embrace even the black flamingo feathers in your life. Like the flamingo feeding upside down, or running on the water's surface... embrace those unique abilities that the Lord has given you personally, and the opportunities that can be yours because you are so beautifully different from others.

I pray you learn to see your business as being his business, and that you can see and accept that he desires to abundantly bless his business that you are stewarding on his behalf.

Remember, you've been brought to the kingdom for such a time as this. God delights in you, has uniquely gifted you, and appointed you to do a special work for him. Your message matters, and you do not need to be afraid.

I want you to write out these verses and meditate on those verses and ask the Lord to help you to not to be afraid.

Psalm 56:3-4

1 Peter 5:7

Isaiah 41:10

Psalm 91:4-5, 10-11

Psalm 119:165

Write out the following verses and meditate on the God who is my Shepherd.

John 10:11, 14

Psalm 100:3

Isaiah 53:6

Psalm 23:1-5

Day six - read *Faith Like Flamingos* Chapter twenty. **Then complete** the following reading and assignment.

Write out the following verses and meditate on the God who forgives.
1 John 1:9
Psalm 86:5
Psalm 103:3, 12

Based on what you've learned about God this week, in your own words create a drawing, song or a prayer of praise to him for who he is.

Based on what you learned about God this week, is there anything in your life or business that you need to change? Make some notes here. Set some deadlines.

In every situation, stop and ask yourself these three questions:
1. What are the facts of the situation?
2. What do I know to be true about my God in this situation?
3. Based on the truths I know, how does my God want me to respond

Let's purpose in our hearts to
1. Be content, but also anticipate growth.
2. Believe he IS who he says he is in his Word.
3. Take captive our thoughts and imaginations and compare them to his Word before accepting them as truth.
4. Embrace the talents and skills, the uniqueness he's given us personally and in our opportunities instead of focusing on our lack.

Day seven - **attend** the discussion class or watch the recording.
Record any notes here.

5.

WEEK FIVE

Day one - **watch** the week five video. **Journal** your thoughts here.

D ay two - read *Faith Like Flamingos* Chapter twenty-one. **Then complete** the following reading and assignment.

—-

Side note: I want to honor you for the effort that you are putting into this study and into your relationship with God and bettering your business abilities. Stick with it. - Katie

—-

If you know me, if you're familiar with some of my other books, then you know that praising God intentionally is a big deal in my life. The Lord has taught me that over and over again, in every situation, I can stop and realize that even in the midst of this, there is something to praise the Lord for.

No matter what it is, no matter how bad it seems, no matter how crazy it seems, even in this, I can praise the Lord.

In "The Sound of Music" Maria von Trapp says, "When one door shuts, somewhere the Lord opens a window." In the midst of any trial I can speak frankly to my Lord: "That door seems like it's barred and bolted. Lord, what do you want me to see in this? Where are you trying to direct my attention? If this is not where I need to go, this looks impossible, but I know you're the God of the impossible. I can praise you for that, even when I don't see how you're going to do this..." There is always something to be thankful for and to praise him for.

When our son was diagnosed with Type 1 juvenile diabetes while I was teaching the **Doing Business With God** course in 2019, we almost lost him.

So many people said, "Oh, I'm so sorry this happened!" and "Oh, how terrible for you all."

We responded with, "No, God is good. This is good. This *gift* God has given us and given to my son will allow us to have conversations and things in common with many more people than we ever could have before." God is *always* good. And we can praise him for the gift of diabetes, because of the opportunities it will bring to share our story for God's glory.

There are three steps I believe to responding correctly to a test or trial. And by the way, God said not to be surprised when we have them:

"Beloved, do not be surprised at the fiery trial when it comes upon you to test you, as though something strange were happening to you. But rejoice insofar as you share Christ's sufferings, that you may also rejoice and be glad when his glory is revealed." 1 Peter 4:12-13.

God is not surprised and he never forces you through a trial by yourself (Hebrews 13:5).

In a trial, first we must give thanks. Write out these verses.

James 1:2

1 Thessalonians 5:18

Second, we must be willing to believe in the sovereignty of God. If he is not surprised and ordained or allowed this for my good or his glory, then, I need to ask "what am I supposed to be seeing here, Lord? Open my eyes to see your goodness, favor and purpose and help me trust even if I can't."

My late mentor Dan Miller exemplified this even to the point that in announcing his late stage cancer diagnosis to friends and family, a few weeks before his death, he was asking and encouraging us to ask "What does this make possible?" What do I need to learn from this? How will this make me better? How could God be using this?

And third, we need to choose to praise him.

Scripture is full of intentional praise being lifted to God in the midst of hard circumstances. The interesting thing about it is that when we choose to lift our eyes out of our downcast spirit and up to his face, when we choose to praise him for the character of God that never changes in spite of the hard he's walking us through, our outlook changes.

"CHANGING YOUR PERSPECTIVE AND ATTITUDE IS THE FIRST STEP TO CHANGING YOUR CIRCUMSTANCE." JEFF TESTERMAN

What negative things in your life or business can you turn around and praise him for? See his goodness in? See the opportunities in?

How does what you know to be true about God, his Word, and yourself help you do this?

Read aloud 1 Peter 1:3-9 and write out verse 7 below.

Write out Hebrews 13:8.

Day three - read *Faith Like Flamingos* Chapter twenty-two. **Then complete** the following reading and assignment.

The power of "failing."

Whoever thought there would be power in failing?

What is the power of failing? It's embracing the process.

I like to say, "There is no failure, only learning forward." God's path to success is often through failing. Why? Because that's when we learn about ourselves and that's when we learn about God—in those hard times. When I'm at the top of my game, at the top of the world, I don't have a need for God.

God often takes us through those valleys so that we get to know Him. Then we can include Him in our next mountaintop experience. There is a quote that says, "to climb a higher mountain you must first come down from the one you're on and cross the valley." Growing a business, just like life, is full of ups and downs.

"THERE IS NO FAILURE, ONLY LEARNING FORWARD."

Think about David and Moses and Jesus and Joseph, and all the things that they went through. It was failure after failure, after failure, from the eyes of men. But when you have God's perspective, when you see God was walking through them each step of the way, when you see God was preparing them for something bigger, then you see how this can also work in your life. Again, rehearsing those histories and rehearsing to yourself the stories of people who have gone on before you gives hope for your own future.

Jeremiah 29:11 tells us God's plans for us are to give us hope and a future. He does that often through the stories of other people. Our response should be to give thanks and to praise him. Ask yourself, "What can I develop or learn in the process of this trial or this failure?" I can still acknowledge that God is good, even in the middle of it. And I realize that this is an ongoing process.

I love the story of Charles Schulz, the author of the *Snoopy* comics, and how he got rejected time after time and told he was no good and that he would never be a writer and all this other stuff. But he persisted and became a world famous cartoonist. And he wrote about his own life and how he persisted in the thing he knew he was supposed to share.

I had an interview with a book agent once who served many top of the line Christian book publishing companies. I paid for the interview, prepared my manuscript and my story pitch, traveled from Mexico to Texas to meet with her only to have her tell me that my idea for what became *In Spite of Myself* was no good, and that no one would read it. She said it wouldn't sell. After nursing my disappointment though, I felt strongly that God wanted me to publish it anyway, and a year and a half later, the Lord allowed us to take that book to market as a self-published book and it to a bestseller status right away.

You have to follow what God says. Get other people's opinions in as much as they matter, and as much as they can be educational and useful for you, but realize that their opinions ultimately are not equal to God's plan for you.

God's plan is always better, always higher. If he has put this in your heart to do, H he e will do it through you.

"Faithful is he that calleth you, who also will do it." 1 Thessalonians 5:24.

Reminding ourselves of what God has done in the past gives hope and courage to our present, and for our future.

Read Joshua 4:5-7.

Write out some examples from Scripture, history or your own story where God has given victory and blessing so that you can remember what he did and recount that in the days you, or your children, need to be reminded of who he is and what he is capable of.

Read aloud and write out the following verses:
Psalm 42:11
1 Thessalonians 5:18

What does God say to give him thanks for?

When I thank him for the circumstance, I am acknowledging his sovereignty in ordaining (making happen on purpose) or allowing this (because it will fulfill a purpose) in my life.
Do you believe God is all-powerful (omnipotent) and all-knowing (omniscient)?

Do you believe he is good and everything he does is good (omni-benevolent)?

Can you take your thoughts captive then to focus enthuse truths, thank him, praise him for who he is and what he's doing (even if you don't see it happening)?

Thanks then, in everything, will help reinforce your beliefs and your thinking, which can then change how you are feeling about the circumstance. Knowing God gives grace (divine enablement in the midst of a the circumstance) and peace.

Day four - read *Faith Like Flamingos* Chapter twenty-three. Then **complete** the following reading and assignment.

I've been reading some secular business books lately, and they echo this natural law of persistence that God has in place. Those who are consistent, those who are persistent, are the ones who set themselves apart in business and are the ones who ultimately win at the end of the day. The difference between a successful person and an unsuccessful person is that one is a quitter who never quit.

I quit about once a month. I go have a cry, remember my why, and come back at it. We all want to quit sometimes. We all have stumbling blocks, we all have speed bumps, we all have roadblocks and disappointments. We all hit a wall, but the difference in the person who wins and succeeds is that they don't let the hard stuff stop them. They keep going. They find a way. They think bigger. They think broader. They find a way to get around the obstacle and keep going. They persist because they have that confidence that this is what God wants me to do, and I will faithfully pursue this calling. I will not stop until I've done it.

THE DIFFERENCE IN THE PERSON WHO WINS AND SUCCEEDS IS THAT THEY DON'T LET THE HARD STUFF STOP THEM.

A 1915 biography called *Thomas Alva Edison* by Francis Rolt-Wheeler reports that one of Edison's young assistant had grown weary of perpetual experiments, thousands of them, which had all failed to reach the desired end. "It's a shame," said this young fellow, petulantly, "that we should have worked all these weeks without getting any results!" "Results!" cried Edison in surprise. "No results? Why, man, I have gotten a lot of results! I know several thousand things that won't work."

That persistence really stands out. But then there's also God's part and our part. Again, bringing in that natural law of how things are supposed to work, combined with the divine enablement that God gives his people to get things done. We should be content, but not so much that we're lazy. We don't want to be lazy in our business. We want to be diligent in our business while also being content with where we are. We want a heart that says, "God, I am thankful for what you've given me. I am grateful for where I am today and I am so looking forward to what you're doing tomorrow and I'm not just going to be content, just sit here and rot, but to keep working towards what I know you have for me even more in the future."

So not being lazy, but being diligent with your work and treating it as work. That means being diligent in returning calls, answering emails, in communication, and being diligent with the numbers and knowing your numbers and in working off of those numbers, diligent in your marketing. And it means being diligent to embrace those trials and say, this is not a trial. It's just a test to see how we're going to respond.

What do I know about God?

Based on that, how does he want me to respond to this difficulty in my business?

Don't blame other people. Take the responsibility for the things that you are responsible for. Learn to be mature in that and to master that. If we don't know how to master ourselves, other people will master us. And that is the absolute truth.

There's a big difference between a temporary setback and failure. God's people are never failures, because with him we can conquer all. Nothing is impossible to our Lord. If he has called you to do it, he will give you what you need to get it done. Winston Churchill said, "Success is going from failure to failure with great enthusiasm."

I want you to think about your business. Think about the "failures" that you've had, which are really obstacles to learn from and overcome, because you are overcoming them.

Think about what it can teach you, and how that makes you better for the next go around.

Think about how you can bring what you know about God into the situation, into the trial, into the setback, into the speed bump, and figure out: "Okay, these are the facts. This is the situation. This is what I know about God. So, based on these truths, what am I going to do? How do I handle this? How does God want me to respond? What's the next step?"

If you can't clearly see the next step, trust the Lord and commit it to him, then you do whatever seems logical as the next right step. Do that one step at a time. Remember, you've been brought to the kingdom for such a time as this. God delights in you, has uniquely gifted you, and appointed you to do a special work for him.

What protections can you establish, so you're not tempted to be lazy in business? lazy in customer service? lazy in honesty?

What systems can you put into place to be more diligent/ persistent with your marketing activities or numbers: accounting, stats, emails, conversion rates, etc?

Day five - read *Faith Like Flamingos* Chapter twenty-four. **Then complete** the following reading and assignment.

God is my judge.

This is big for many believers who are in business because not only does it have to do with me and my judgement towards other people, but it also has to do with how I receive criticism, comments, suggestions, and help.

I can pass judgment on those things, or I can take them to the Lord and say, "Okay, this is what they're saying, God, what do you say?" Then go back and compare that to Scripture.

God is the judge. He's the only one I have to please. I only have to please him. If God is happy with me, I'm good. I don't need any human permission or approval to obey the voice of God. If you're married, there is a partner in that equation. According to Scripture you are one flesh and you have to take that into consideration. But ultimately, those are only two people that you need to please. Those are the only two people that you need to be sure that what you're doing aligns with what they want you to do.

My God is my judge, not my random blog readers, not the random commenters on social media, not customers who are unhappy because they didn't read the instructions to do something right, and now I've got to fix their problem, not long distance family who are neither involved in or the right fit client for my business... God is my judge, not those other people.

My heart needs to be one that is always looking to serve God, because he is the one I'm going to give an answer to for what I do in business and for how I respond and how I love people, even those people who are judging me. I don't have to let them be my judge, and I don't have to take on the responsibility of being their judge. I don't have to read into situations. I can just look at the facts and make an un-emotional decision. I can choose not to get emotionally involved with other people's problems or issues, because I'm not their judge. I can pray for them, I can empathize with them, but I don't have to let it ruin my day or control my thinking because I am not their judge. God is the one who is ultimately going to judge their actions and "drama."

It is very freeing when you know God as the righteous and good judge of you and other people, because it takes the guilt that other people try to place on you, off of you. It also takes the responsibility off of you for having to judge other people. It's a win win to let God be the judge of all.

IT'S A WIN WIN TO LET GOD BE THE JUDGE OF ALL.

The Greatest Salesman in the World by OG Mandino, is an excellent book for Christians in business, and it's one of the books I often recommend to folks in our marketing membership program. One of the biggest things that the book teaches is loving (not judging) other people. In the book, the main character says:

"I will greet this day with love in my heart. They may refuse to buy from me, but I will show them love. They may refuse my speech, they may refuse my dress. They may not like the way that I talk or offer things or what I do, but they cannot refuse the love that shines through me."

That, my friend, is how we can bring Christ authentically into the marketplace. Your willingness to love other people sets you apart and makes you different, desirable even. This is huge. God wants me to love and serve others because he is the ultimate example of that love and service. I don't have to love what they do. I don't have to love what they stand for. I don't have to love what they are or what they promote in their personal life. But I do need to show them the love of Christ that says, I'm not your judge. I'm just here to support you and help you take the next right step. How can I help?

I should practice discernment. I do want to be humble and helpful when God presents an opportunity to help someone else see truth, but never with a judgmental spirit, or a motive-reading, critical spirit. I can't fix anything. Only can can restore, renew and revive.

Those are awesome principles when you see who God is and then ask how that applies to you and your business.

YOUR WILLINGNESS TO LOVE OTHER PEOPLE SETS YOU APART AND MAKES YOU DIFFERENT.

Read aloud and write out 1 Peter 1:2

God is the judge of me; I only need to please him.

God is the judge of others; I can let him handle their case when they wrong me or wrongly judge me.

God is the judge of others; it's not my place or responsibility to pass judgement on them.

Here are other verses to read and meditate on concerning God is my judge.
2 Corinthians 5;10
Galatians 6:7-8
Hebrews 9:27
1 Corinthians 4:4-5
Romans 14:10-12
Revelation 20:12-13
Psalm 50:4, 6
Psalm 37:1-11
Romans 12:19
James 4:11-12
Romans 14:10-, 12-13
Luke 6:36-37
Matthew 7:1-5
Hebrews 4:12
1 Peter 4:8-9

Day six - read the final chapter of *Faith Like Flamingos*
Chapter twenty-five.
Then complete the following reading and assignment.

The power of the love of God.

1 Corinthians 13 tells us that the greatest of all of our possible actions is love in action. The word charity in that chapter is translated literally as "love in action".

A key part of blending our faith into our business is what we do. It's showing love in action, to team, to partners, to clients and the world at large.

"So also faith by itself, if it does not have works, is dead. But someone will say, "You have faith and I have works." Show me your faith apart from your works, and I will show you my faith by my works." James 2:17-18.

I know you might be thinking "Well, but I don't know how much to show my faith in my business? How much do I talk about my faith? Or how much do I need to make it obvious and blatant in my business?"

I would say it's probably different for everyone. You're going to have to let the Holy Spirit guide you and tell you how much. You've got to talk with him, to seek his glory. Let him show you. Ask for his wisdom. He'll show you.

My friend an artist and business mentor to artists, Matt Tommey said once "I was so worried about when people come into my art studio, what do I do, God? Do I need to just drop everything and go witness to them? Because I want to be back over here, making art. He said, it was like God told him, "You just need to love the people and let me change the people." And he said, "I truly believe that God's Holy Spirit is powerful enough to speak through my baskets and sculptures and to heal them or to otherwise influence their lives."

God can work through inanimate things. God can work through art that He inspires you to create. He can work through food that shows his love to someone. He can work through the sweet spirit of a mechanic. He can work through principles online. He can work through the written words of your story or the spoken words of your instruction. Or even through the attitude with which you deliver your product or coaching. You let him work. Don't put limits on how the Holy Spirit can use you. Let God do the work through you (1 These. 5:24).

The other question I get a lot is, "What if God asked me to serve someone who I know is in sin?"

My answer to this tends to be a bit sarcastic when I'm not full of the spirit. I want to say "Well, my goodness. Do you think God would ask you to show his love to somebody who was in sin?! I mean, where do we see that in Scripture? How dare God ask us to reach out to someone who is in sin and show them love?" That's sarcastic of course, but the obvious answer is God showed his love to people in sin over and over again! Including you and I! Jesus ate with sinners, traveled with them, fed them, healed them, *loved* them. And so should we if we want to be like Jesus.

The woman at the well, the woman caught in adultery, the lepers, the lame man, the tax collector, the 5,000 and their families... What about you and me? We were in sin before he saved us. He showed his love to us. Why would we refuse to show his love to someone who was in sin? Our sin is no different. There are no grade reports on your sin level. Every single sin is just as stinky in the nose of God as any other sin.

You're no better than they are, and yet God did this for you. How could you not serve them and show his love to them over and over and over?

"LOVING THEM IS A LIFE AND DEATH MATTER."

Christian business owners so often ask, "But, What if I don't agree? What if I don't like the way they live? How can I serve them?" You can serve them because God served you, bought you, redeemed you, and now lives in you. You may be the only person who shows them the love of God.

How cool would that be? If you loved them and you got a chance to share Jesus with them and he changed their life, loving them is a life and death matter.

There are lots of Christians who can refuse to serve people, but *you* have been called to love.

"THERE ARE LOTS OF CHRISTIANS WHO CAN REFUSE TO SERVE PEOPLE, BUT *YOU* HAVE BEEN CALLED TO LOVE."

A person is not defined by their sin. We don't love the *sin*. Jesus didn't love the sin either, but he never refused to love the person. God doesn't love our sin, he loves us in spite of it. Love them into a relationship with him.

I have been to so many business events in our years of business that were secular events. Some of them are really high ticket events, CEOs of million dollar companies, and not a single one have I gone to where there wasn't someone—sometimes multiple people—at that event who would come up to me and say, "What is it about you? You just radiate light. I walked by you and just felt this peace. What is that?"

It gave me an opportunity to tell them, "It's Jesus. Do you know who he is? Can I tell you about him?" I have shared Christ with agnostics, shamans and millionaires. How many of you could imagine being at a secular event and having a chance to go up and ask how their business was doing?

"Hey, I appreciate that you're here to improve your business. How can I help you today?" I'm interested in them as a person because I know God loves them. And if this person can do that well with a business that serves the enemy, think what he could do if God got ahold of his heart. Do you see how this can make an impact?

You're not just called to serve in a little bubble. You're called to serve in the world. Jesus says, I am sending them into the world because the world needs to know Jesus. And they're not going to know him if you refuse to love them through the things that you do,

If you are that one person who will love them, because God loves them you will win a chance to talk to them about the most important thing in their life. That brings glory to God that gives the business owner a good name.

God doesn't care about the profits. He owns everything... He cares about the people. Remember, money is just a tool to him. Money is just something that allows you to do more and reach more people so that you can share this message with more people.

If there are situations where you truly believe that you cannot serve, and that you cannot do this in good conscience, (I think sometimes there are situations like that.) I believe the Holy Spirit is there to give you wisdom. If you will think about this in advance, put policies in place in your business, and give yourself time to get to know clients and their situations, then the Holy Spirit can help you figure out ways to still honor God and love them well while not participating in their sin.

Maybe there is a schedule conflict. Maybe this is not the right timing. Maybe there is someone who could better serve them. Not just refusing someone, but something like, "I can't do this right now, but how can I serve them? If it's not me, then who can I recommend that could help them?" The Holy Spirit is there to give wisdom.

So that even then, you're obeying the Spirit by not participating with them, but you're also not offending them while standing for your own values. You're not burning any bridges that might prohibit you from reaching them with the gospel in the future.

Love is not a feeling. Love is an action. We feel loved when we've been the recipient of an action. We feel loved when someone speaks well to us, spends time with us, gifs us something, listens to us, does something for us, touches us in a special way... Love is an action.

Even God's love is an action: "But God shows his love for us in that while we were sinners, Christ died for us." Romans 5:8 (ESV).

"If ye love me, keep my commandments." John 14:5. Love is shown by our actions.

We say we love someone, but that love is not validated until an action validates it.

Read aloud 1 Corinthians 13:4-7 and replace the word *charity* or *love* with the words *love in action.*

Write out below the 15 things that love does from 1 Corinthians 13:4-7

1.
2.
3.
4.
5.
6.
7.
8.
9.
10.
11.
12.
13.
14.
15.

How does thinking about love as an action change the way you will interact with family members, friends, readers, customers, service providers, and even competitors?

1 Corinthians 13:8 says "Love never fails." What does this mean to you in the context of love being an action?

Read aloud and write out Proverbs 3:27.

Read aloud and write out Galatians 6:2, and 10

How does thinking about this command to "love one another" and the list of actions love takes (above) change the way you will live generously in your life and business?

Why must we have love (love in action)? Again, it's not about us, it's to give testimony of God. Read aloud and write out John 13;35.

How does today's discussion apply to you and your business when you see God as the owner and yourself as a CEO?

How do I continue to make God, the owner of the business, look good in the world through this work that I'm doing?

Based on what you've learned about God this week, is there anything in your life or business that you need to change? Make some notes here. Set some deadlines.

In every situation, stop and ask yourself these three questions:
1. What are the facts of the situation?
2. What do I know to be true about my God in this situation?
3. Based on the truths I know, how does my God want me to respond

Let's purpose in our hearts to
1. Repent where necessary of resentfulness, unfair judgements and unbelief.
2. Believe he IS who he says he is in his Word.
3. Take captive our thoughts and imaginations, purposing in our hearts to believe Truth over emotion in every circumstance.
4. Embrace the trial as a good thing from his hand and be ready to thank him for it and learn from it.
5. Love others, not just in word, but with actions that prove his love for them.

Day seven - **attend** the discussion class or watch the recording.
Record any notes here.

6.

WEEK SIX

Day one - **watch** the week six video.
Journal your thoughts here.

Day two - **complete** the following reading and assignment.

"YOUR LIFE DOES NOT GET BETTER BY CHANCE, IT GETS BETTER BY CHANGE." -KATIE HORNOR, *FAITH LIKE FLAMINGOS*

The Tool of Time

Are you changing beliefs that were holding you back or holding you hostage? Changing your thoughts about yourself and the unique gifts you bring to the world? Changing your thoughts about your business and the possibilities for growth when you see it and run it as God's business? Changing your thoughts about selling to and serving your people?

The thing that I specifically want you to look at is the change in your definition of success. What is your definition of success today? Write it down, without looking at what you wrote earlier, when we talked about this back in week one. I want you to write today what success means to you and what your definition of success is now.

Success is....

Now, go back and compare it to what you wrote in chapter one and see if that definition has changed. See if what God has done in you is reflected in that new definition. You should also realize that your definition of success even today is going to continue to change, because God is going to continue to work in you and continue to fulfill in you that work that he has started and promises to complete in you until the day of Jesus Christ (Philippians 1:6).

In this study so far we've seen who God is and how we apply that to every situation in business. We've learned to apply that to decisions, to offenses, and priorities... Now we're going to learn to master our time and our focus for the glory of God.

"IT'S NOT ABOUT CONTROLLING YOUR TIME, IT'S ABOUT CONTROLLING YOUR NO'S."-JEFF TESTERMAN, *BIBLE BASED BUSINESS*

I believe that time is just as much a tool as treasure and team can be. The difference is that time is more precious because we can't ever get it back once used and we can't create more of it. We have to use it intentionally.

In the Mastermind group I lead, I have taken our members through the book *Deep Work*, by Cal Newport. The central idea is that the reason that we don't have time for the things that are important is we have over-committed to things that are not important, but we can't set them aside and focus on those things that are supposed to be priorities.

So let me ask you: "Where are you over committed?"

Time management begins in your heart. Remember that all of your thoughts and your actions are based on what you believe, so, it starts in your heart. It starts with what you believe. If you believe God does all things well, and if you believe God has given you a sound mind, and if you believe he has given you the ability to manage the things he's put in your hand well, then he can help you handle time management too. If you need his wisdom to do that, all you have to do is ask (James 1:5). And if you need his help to do that, he promises to do through you the things he's called you to do (1 Thess. 5:24). So you really are set up for success from day one!

Time management starts with what do I believe about God, about the time that he's given me, and about the tasks he has given me? We must evaluate all of that.

Start by evaluating your tasks. What do you have on your plate right now? And how many of those are *God given* assignments vs. things that you just committed to or took responsibility for on your own without consulting him?

It's sobering, but I want you to take time to think through what your commitments are right now, personally and professionally? Write them down.

Mark the ones that were God given.

Next, go through and cross off the ones that you know you need to get rid of.

These are things you *know* you don't even need to pray about, because you know that you're not supposed to be doing that. Get rid of them.

You *do* need to keep your word and you need to have integrity even in the way you cancel those commitments. However, it can be done.

As for wisdom, if you're married, ask your spouse, if not a trusted mentor, to help you figure out how you can get out of that commitment or pass that task off to somebody else who can be responsible for it. God will give you wisdom and get those things off your plate.

Next, mark the ones that you think you need to get rid of, but you're not sure about them. Ask God for clarity. He will give you clarity about what does not need to be on your plate. Narrow down the things that you don't need to do.

I believe that time management can be spiritual warfare because even good things become bad if they distract us, or if they keep us from doing the main things that God wants us to do. The enemy of your soul knows that it feels good to be busy doing good things and that he can use that as a powerful distractor from God's best for you. Be careful!

Can you see evidence of time management being spiritual warfare in your life?

D

ay three - complete the following reading and assignment.

Manage Your no's.

Managing your no's is your first line of defense in honoring God with the tool of time. Some call it evaluating opportunity cost. Does this opportunity line up with your goals and commitments for your business? If not, then this is not the time.

Why do we set goals and commitments for our quarter and our month and our week? It's so that we know what we're supposed to be focused on. If an opportunity presents itself, that is a wonderful opportunity I've got to go back to the drawing board, back into discussion with the Owner of the business and I've got to say, "Okay, God, does this line up with the goals that you had me set for this week?" If not, then I've got to say, "No, I can't do that right now." I do not have the space. I do not have the time. I do not have the schedule, whatever it is, to focus on the stated goal and give this opportunity the attention that it needs. So I'm going to have to say no for right now.

Remember, every no doesn't necessarily mean no forever. It just means no right now. This is true whether you're asking something and you receive a no, or whether someone is asking of you and you have to give a no.

That no can be very freeing for you because you have the confidence of the goals and the commitments that God has set before you as priorities. Compare these opportunities to that set of commitments and goals and say, does this line up with what God wants me to be focused on right now? And if not, then you don't need to do it.

For instance, I was in the middle of a certain marketing class and the opportunity came up to take a second one. I knew I needed the second one, but wouldn't be able to give adequate time to both, so I said "No for now" to the second one, finished the first class and the next time the second class came around I could embrace it and focus on excelling in applying that content to my business. I was focused on one thing at a time, both intellectually and financially, whereas if I'd done both at once, it would have been stressful in both areas.

It is possible to be very busy and yet so distracted that you're not worth anything. Then you're not getting anything done well. That's the power of *The 12 Week Year*, by Brian Moran. It's the idea behind the *Flamingo Biz Planner,* the a quarterly planner I created. These two books help you learn to focus on those short-term goals and get them done. You can be much more effective that way than if you are focused on ten different long-term goals and trying to do a little on each of them all at the same time.

When you focus on short-term goals, you can focus on one main goal, commit and get in there and give it your full concentration. You can get it done and then move on to the next thing. You're much more effective and productive than if your time was distracted in between everything that you're trying to get done in a long-term plan.

Think about the things that are burdening you. God's burden is light (Matt. 11:30). God says his ways are not burdensome to us. If you have a responsibility that has become a mental burden to you, then you need to take that to the Lord and ask him for wisdom and clarity. "Lord, you said your ways are not burdensome. If this is what you have for me to do, then why am I feeling this way? Is it something I need to change? Is it my attitude? Is it my perspective? Is it something I need to give up and stop doing because joy is not there? You said your ways were not burdensome. Help me know." That doesn't mean we have to be happy, go lucky and bounce off the walls while we're doing it, right? But we shouldn't dread those things that the Lord has asked us to do. It may not be easy, but there shouldn't be a dread for it if it's something in the Lord's will for you.

Go back and ask the Lord about those things and try to figure out where that problem lies. Is it with you? Is it with someone else? Is it something that you can get out of? Is it your attitude or your perspective that needs to change? A change of perspective may allow you to see those things as from his hand and to see them as a joy and not a burden.

You should also know that your saying 'no' is going to offend some people, so plan on it. Jeff Testerman says, "They will accuse you of being lazy. They will accuse you of being uncaring. They may even say you are in sin if you don't do what they're asking you to do." However, he says to you, "Close your ears to those accusations, you turn your ear to the still small voice of your God. He will tell you which way to walk and what commitments to take on."

My friend, as you have completed this study, you have also been learning to know your God, learning to go to him and say, "What is the truth? What do I know about God? What does he want me to do?" He will lead you in your decisions and in your commitments and in your saying no to things that are not his best.

Is it hard for you to say no? why or why not?

What truth/s do you need to meditate on to strengthen your "no" muscle?

D ay four - complete the following reading and assignment.

Discern God's voice

As a child of God, we need to be in the Word to know his principles for living and business, but we also need to develop discernment and awareness of his still small voice telling us what we're supposed to be doing. When we're so busy and so distracted that we have no time to listen for his voice, or to stop and think that we even need to ask him about something, then we're too busy.

Others may be offended by your commitment to hear and follow God. They may think whatever they're going to think. Let them judge. What is important is that you recognize and obey the voice of God, that you are pleasing him with your decisions - even when it means saying no.

That might be a disappointment to someone else who does not understand, or who does not have your relationship with God. They are not you. You can't judge them. They should not be judging you, but it's not for you to judge them because they shouldn't be judging you. It just goes around in a circle and nobody gets anywhere. So don't let it bother you. Don't take it personally. You need to do what you know God wants you to do. You're going to answer for you, not for them.

You can probably envision that person you know who is busy, busy, busy, busy, busy all the time? They're so busy, they can't even have dinner with their family. They always have an activity. They've always got something on the calendar, and if they don't, they're looking for something to fill that space.

Over so many years of working in ministry and with clients, I've realized that one reason we might be tempted to fill up our calendar with busy-ness because we're afraid of the thing God wants us to do. I'm not saying that's the case every time, but I know some people who have been like that. I've been

121

that way myself. You have a deadline looming, so what do you do? Everything but the thing you're supposed to be doing. Am I right? We do everything: "Oh look, my bed needs to be made." "Oh look, nobody did the laundry yet today. I need to go do that." Even though it's my teen's job. "Oh look, I should clean out my thousands of emails in my inbox, that's not bothered me for six months, but now that I don't want to do this other thing today is the day." Am I right?

When I have a deadline, it seems like everything else is more important. That's because I have something making me afraid of getting that done.

You and I need to attack those fears with our actions. We need to sit down and figure out what the next right step is, and then do it. In Matthew 25, in the story of the talents, the servant who received the most reward went out quickly and took action. Perhaps he had the most experience and knew that he had a window of opportunity? It didn't say he wasn't afraid. It did say he quickly took action. You and I when we know what needs to be done, need to act quickly, not sit frozen in fear.

What is that thing you're afraid of?

Why are you afraid of it? Go deeper. Why are you afraid of that? Go deeper.

Why are you afraid of that? Go deep and keep going as deep as you can.

They say to go even as many as seven questions deep for why you are afraid of doing this thing to get to the real root problem.

Then attack the root problem of that fear. Is it a fear of man? Is it that you don't know how? What is it? Let's take action to get that thing done and cross it off your list.

What task are you resisting right now?

Why are you afraid of it?

Why are you afraid of that?

Why are you afraid of that?

Why are you afraid of that?

Why?

Why?

Why?

Read aloud and write out 2 Timothy 1:7.

What has God given us according to that passage?
1.
2.
3.

Day five - **complete** the following reading and assignment.

Develop Powerful Focus.

So many times we fill our lives with busy-ness to distract us from the one thing that we need to be doing, that we really, really need to get done. Luke chapter 10 tells the story of Martha and Mary. You may have heard this over and over and over again, but I want you to think about it from this aspect of being so busy that you don't have the time to do that one key thing right now.

"As they went on their way, Jesus entered a village and a woman named Martha welcomed him into her house (Luke 10:38), and she had a sister called Mary who sat at the Lord's feet and listened to his teaching, but Martha was distracted with much serving." It actually says distracted there in the ESV. I love that it says she is actually "distracted with much serving" (Luke 10:40, ESV). "She went to him and said, Lord, do you not care that my sister has left me to serve alone? Tell her then to help me. And the Lord answered "Martha. Martha, you are anxious and you're troubled about so many things, but one thing is necessary and Mary has chosen that good portion which will not be taken away from her."

Martha was busy *serving!* She was doing a *good thing* and it was a distraction. She was so busy serving that she was completely distracted from the one thing she should have been focused on, sitting at Jesus' feet.

Mary was sitting at his feet. Martha was in the other room. She was all over the house. She was welcoming people. She was loving on people. I want you to understand this. God was not reprimanding her for serving. Martha was loving on people. He corrected her because she was allowing the good thing to keep her from the first priority.

Her reputation as hostess and her relationship to her guests had become a distraction from the one relationship that mattered most, and from the activity she knew she

125

should have been doing at that minute, which was sitting at Jesus' feet.

How many times do you and I get so busy that it distracts us from our first love, from our highest priority: relationship with God, sitting at his feet and learning about him? How often does serving and doing good for others keep me from knowing him better and become a distraction from what He wants me to do? If Martha had known God, if she had been close enough to hear his voice in that moment, she would have known that the most important thing was learning of him, and getting to know him so that when he was not at her house teaching, she could serve those people and meet their needs better.

We cannot let ourselves be so distracted by the good busy-ness that we neglect knowing Christ, because knowing him is key to more grace and more peace (2 Peter 1:2).

Knowing that you have God's peace, his divine enablement, power, love and sound mind, think about the things you wrote about being fearful of doing yesterday. Write out below the simple step by step tasks you need to do to complete the task and date you'll do it.

Day six - complete the following reading and assignment.

The Freedom of Relationship

It's in knowing God that we learn he doesn't want me to be afraid. He is my judge. He doesn't want me to judge others. And when I'm loving and serving others, God is my counselor.

Who is the one I run to when I have a problem? Do I run to my friends? Do I run to Facebook and ask the social world? Or do I run to God, who is the great counselor? He is the one with all the answers, the one who knows me inside and out. God wants you to go to him with your problems because he is your Counselor. He is the one that can give you knowledge and wisdom and understanding.

"Being confident of this very thing, that he which hath begun a good work in you will perform it until the day of Jesus Christ." (Philippians 1:6)

He's the one doing the work in your life, not your Facebook friends. I'm not saying you shouldn't have Facebook friends, but we don't need to be whining all over Facebook about our problems. That doesn't help anybody. We need to take our problems to the Lord. Take it to the Lord in prayer, listen for him and what he has to say.

"Lord, what do you want me to learn about you right now in this hard time? What do you want to teach me? What do you want me to share with others? How do you want me to respond? What's my next right step?

He promises wisdom. If I ask him, he wants me to come near to sit at his feet and to let him be my Counselor. Let him train me how to serve those people better. God is with me. He is with me everywhere. He's with me in the dark. He's with me in the daylight. He's with me and my business. He's with me in my home, in my car, and my bed (Hebrews 13:5).

It doesn't matter where I am. The Lord is always with me, and those verses reassure me that he is always with me. Think about Psalm 23: "When I walk through the Valley of the

Shadow of Death, I will fear no evil for you are with me." Those shadows are just shadows when we walk with Christ, because he is more powerful.

Your God is omnipresent. Did you forget? He's omnipresent. He's omniscient, powerful, omnipotent. He's got more power than anything that's lurking in those shadows, and he's walking with you, protecting you every step of the way. You may not understand it now, just how he protects. You may not even see it until you get to glory. But the Lord is there. He is ever powerful. All powerful, ever present with you. He is there—an ever present help in times of trouble (Psalm 46:1).

"And the Lord, he it is that doth go before thee; he will be with thee, he will not fail thee, neither forsake thee: fear not, neither be dismayed" Deuteronomy 31:8.

"Fear thou not; for I am with thee: be not dismayed; for I am thy God: I will strengthen thee; yea, I will help thee; yea, I will uphold thee with the right hand of my righteousness." Isaiah 41:10.

We have a righteous God who promises to be with us every single situation he's asked us to walk through. My God is God. Psalm 100:3 says, "Know ye that the Lord he is God."

This entire study has been based on the fact that we need to *know* God, and when we know him, as I Peter 1:2 says, we will have multiplied measures of grace and peace in the knowledge of who he is. We will have that divine enablement, that divine favor, unmerited favor, favor we don't even deserve. When we know who God is, the favor, the enablement, the help, comes from God who says, "I called you to this. I'm going to do it through you. I'm going to give you what you need to get through this."

The peace that passes all understanding (Phil 4:7), and the sound mind that it is in Christ (2 Tim. 1:7). All of that comes when we know our God, not when we're distracted, not when we're running here and there and don't even have time to think or hear his voice. It comes through knowing him by sitting at his feet, through doing studies like this one, and through consciously reminding yourself every day and in every situation, to ask,

1. "What do I know about my God?" Then
2. Based on that, "How does he want me to respond? What is the next right step in my life? In my business? In my family and my marriage, or with my kids? With my grocery budget? With my business funds?"

"KNOWING GOD IS FREEDOM."

Knowing God is freedom, my friend. That is what God is saying when he says that he will give you grace and peace and that it would be multiplied to you in the knowledge of God. You will have the confidence that says, "I only have to please him. Only God needs to be happy with me." That is freedom, and that is what I hope you have found as you've gotten to know God better in this process of hearing from him and gaining confidence to make your business decisions based on his purpose for you, and his calling on your life in alignment with the holy spirit's leading.

When you see God as the owner of your business, and your self as the CEO, president, director or whatever other title you want to give yourself under him, you can

1. Confidently go to him for wisdom in making decisions (James 1:5).
2. Ask for his grace, divine enablement, to focus on the task at hand (1 These. 5:24).
3. Make confident decisions about commitments and distractions because this is his business and you are in charge of working it and growing it with his best interests at heart (1 for. 4:1-2).

4. Rest in the knowledge of him and the peace of mind he gives when we seek him first in our business (2 Peter 1:2).

"YOU DO WHAT YOU DO AND YOU SAY WHAT YOU SAY BECAUSE YOU THINK WHAT YOU THINK, AND YOU THINK WHAT YOU THINK BECAUSE YOU BELIEVE WHAT YOU BELIEVE ABOUT GOD AND HIS WORD AND YOURSELF." - KEN COLLIER

So let me ask you: Are there things you need to quit doing, even in regards to how you safeguard your work or family time, in order to be focused on the things God wants you to do?

After having gone through this study, has your definition of success changed?

Has your relationship with God changed? If so, how?

Has your outlook on your position and responsibilities in your business changed? If so, how?

The answer to wrong actions and words is taking captive every thought and comparing it to, forcing yourself to think according to the truths of Scripture.

Only when we know God can we believe his truth and walk in his power and divine enablement (grace) and favor (grace) and have the peace that is rest and a sound, confident, un-stressed mind. Only when we study his truth and purposefully pursue relationship with him, can we know him.

In every situation, stop and ask yourself these three questions:
1. What are the facts of the situation?
2. What do I know to be true about my God in this situation?
3. Based on the truths I know, how does my God want me to respond, act, speak, decide, love, etc?

This power of knowing God combined with the practice of applying it to your everyday life and business = wisdom. And the wisdom that is from above is what will change your life! (James 3:16-18).

Day seven - attend the discussion class or watch the recording.
Record any notes here.

CONNECT WITH KATIE

Katie Hornor is known as the "Flamingo Lady" because she's uncovered the magnificence of this unique bird, who lives in community, is bold enough not to cower in front of predators, and has its own unique voice. Katie uses the flamingo as a metaphor to coach entrepreneurs to be more confident, create community and leverage their unique voice in the marketplace without compromising family, faith or values.

Katie and her husband Tap have been foreign missionaries since 2007 in México, homeschooling their five kids, speaking and writing business and devotional books and coaching entrepreneurs in business and marketing strategies that honor God and his purpose for them as light in a secular world. Learn more at www.TheFlamingoAdvantage.com/about

Katie's Speaker website: www.KatieHornor.com
email: Katie@TheFlamingoAdvantage.com.com

Share the **Doing Business with God** program with a friend at
    www.BusinessWIthGod.Online

Pick up Katie's Best-selling books at
https://TheFlamingoAdvantage.com.com/books

Katie author page on amazon is
https://amzn.to/3EDIsB2

FOLLOW KATIE ON SOCIAL:
Podcast:
www.TheFlamingoAdvantage.com.com/podcast

Youtube:
www.youtube.com/@KatieHornorFlamingoAdvantage

Facebook:
www.facebook.com/katiehornorvisionary

Free FB group:
www.theflamingosanctuary.com

Instagram:
www.instagram.com/katiehornor
Use #BusinessWithGod to share your review of this program.

LinkedIn:
www.linkedin.com/in/katiehornor/

RECOMMENDED

RESOURCES

Other books by Katie Hornor:
The Flamingo Advantage: How to Leverage Unique, Stay Relevant and Change the World
In Spite of Myself: How Intentional Praise Can Transform Your Heart and Home
Flamingo Biz Planner

Recommended Books:
Bible Based Business by Jeff Testerman
What Do I Know About My God? by Mardi Collier
The Marketplace Christian by Darren Shearer
God's Plan for Living by Matt Tommey
Launch by Jeff Walker
An Understanding Heart by Dan Miller
The Greatest Salesman in the World by Og Mandino
The 12 Week Year by Brian Moran
God Owns My Business by Stanley Tam

Made in the USA
Monee, IL
07 February 2024